SETTING UP IN BUSINESS

Setting Up in Business

An Information Guide

Ray Prytherch and Suzanne Stanley

Gower
Aldershot · Brookfield USA · Hong Kong · Singapore · Sydney

© Ray Prytherch and Suzanne Stanley 1989

All rights reserved. No part of this publication may be reproduced, stored in a retrieval system, or transmitted in any form or by any means, electronic, mechanical, photocopying, recording, or otherwise without the prior permission of the publisher.

Published by
Gower Publishing Company Limited
Gower House
Croft Road
Aldershot
Hants GU11 3HR
England

Gower Publishing Company
Old Post Road
Brookfield
Vermont 05036
USA

Printed in Great Britain by
Billing & Sons Ltd, Worcester

British Library Cataloguing in Publication Data
Prytherch, R. J. (Raymond John), *1945–*
   Setting up in business
   1. Great Britain. Small firms.
   Organisation. Information sources
   I. Title II. Stanley, Suzanne
   III. Series
   658′.022′07041

ISBN 0 566 035731

Contents

	Preface	vii
1	Introduction	1
2	Education and training for small businesses	5
	College-based courses 7	
	The Training Agency 9	
	Other training facilities 11	
3	Self-help guides	14
	General works on starting up and running a small business 14	
	Home-based and part-time opportunities 17	
	Cooperatives and franchises 18	
	Specific aspects of starting and running a small business 20	
4	Opportunities in specific trades and services	27
5	Reference materials	30
	Dictionaries and encyclopaedias 30	
	Directories and handbooks 31	
6	Periodical publications	34
7	Automation and the small business	38
8	The legal requirements	40
	Form of the business 41	
	Choice of premises 42	
	Trading and licensing regulations 43	
	Insurance 43	
	Employment of staff 44	

      Health and safety 46
      Inland Revenue and National Insurance requirements 47
      VAT 48
      Patents, copyright, trade marks and registered designs 49
      In conclusion 50
9 Further sources of advice and support   52
      Government services 53
      National agencies 55
      Commercial assistance 57
      Enterprise agencies and science parks 57
      Local authority services 58
      Other local support 58
      Facts and figures 59
      Pensions for the self-employed 60
      Support for young people 60
      Self-employed disabled people 61
      Support for cooperatives 61
      Professional advisers 61

Index   63

Preface

The intention of this volume in the Information Guide series is to offer guidance on the large range of publications and other resources currently available that give advice on setting up in business. Our material includes self-help guides, reference materials, leaflets from support organizations, information on training and educational courses, government and local authority initiatives. We hope that those intending to start a business, either as a one-person, home-based enterprise, or as a partner in a small company, or joining in a cooperative, or taking up a franchise opportunity will find this book helpful and relevant. Its relevance will also extend to small firms or traders who wish to expand, take on staff, move premises, change their legal status or raise more capital.

Careers advisers and librarians will appreciate its evaluation of numerous apparently similar guides and find contact suggestions for many other sources of material.

We should like to acknowledge the help given to us by friends and colleagues; we also appreciate the courtesy of James Askew and Son Ltd of Preston, in allowing us access to their showroom collection.

Ray Prytherch
Suzanne Stanley

September 1988

# 1

Introduction

UK statistics show an extraordinary growth in the number of self-employed people and small businesses; of the employed population of the country, one in nine is self-employed – which is four times the ratio ten years ago. Other statistics are less reliable, and tell a less optimistic story: one third of new enterprises are reckoned to fail within the first two years. Not all new businesses need to register for VAT purposes, but of those that do 26 per cent fail within two years: this is one of the few figures that is better than guesswork on the success rate. As a comparison, in the United States 80 per cent of new small businesses fail over five years, so that we may consider the British figures represent fair overall success.

The positive side of the picture is therefore that two-thirds of new ventures are successful, or at least remain in being and provide adequate income to their proprietors. There may well be problems over the *quality* of new UK businesses: is there too much optimism and expectation of the rewards of self-employment so that marginal activities are set up that cannot realistically be expected to survive, expand and compete? The government has led the way in simplifying bureaucracy and offering inducement to encourage enterprise and entrepreneurialism; clearly, from a political viewpoint, this helps to ease unemployment from the declining traditional industries, and is in line with the philosophy that tomorrow's prosperity is built on the energy and vision of individuals today.

Other factors have also made self-employment feasible: skills previously could be acquired only by apprenticeship or formal training, but the skills needed for a modern small enterprise can be learned much more readily from open learning courses, run at a time and at a pace to suit the individual learner and often with financial support from government or local authorities. New technological developments make possible sophisticated operations in the home or small office; E-mail, Fax, answerphones, cellular phones and microcomputers make communication and complex clerical activities easy and inexpensive.

The categories of people who now consider self-employment fall principally into four groups: there are those who genuinely want to be on their own in business, hard workers with a deep personal commitment who have an idea in mind and are excited by the planning and resourcing of their scheme; secondly, there are those who are compelled by circumstances (the 'shock theory') to investigate setting up on their own, people who have been made redundant, relocated by firms, or who have been unable to find employment, people whose personal or family circumstances make a home-based career attractive or essential; the third category are those led into this consideration by publicity for financial and other support offered by local authorities, development agencies or government-funded schemes, and who feel they could have a 'better' life by this means than their present one; fourthly, there are those who come in reluctantly for negative reasons, who cannot cope with employee-status, and are running *from* something else rather than *into* self-employment. The most positive stand to gain most from their efforts.

Unlike a conventional job where an interview is the normal selection process, 'applicants' for self-employment select themselves; an examination of oneself, one's personality, needs, motives, resources and strategy is probably the single most important action that can be taken. It is essential to think hard about what self-employment will mean, the commitment that must be there, the analysis of skills and knowledge possessed, a recognition of the high demands on the individual, the element of risk and the pitfalls of over-optimism. Strategy and planning begin with the individual, and then focus on the enterprise, the market, the demand and the resources. Failure at the first attempt should not be followed by despair, but by a second or third strategy; fear

Introduction

of failure is another characteristic to be considered in a realistic plan.

Success in self-employment depends on the time and care taken over preparation and investigation; risks must be recognized – self-respect, health, family life, personal savings; workload and finance must be adequately assessed, problems must be foreseen – irregular income, long hours, loneliness, uncertainty. Moral support from family and friends should be sought and examined before the outset; professional advisers should be carefully heeded; specialist help should be taken into account even at a cost. It is important to avoid isolation, but to listen, discuss, take advice, accept guidance, change plans, monitor progress, and above all adopt an impartial and utterly realistic stance towards the enterprise.

Where should one start? Publishers have noted the upturn in interest and the lure of government schemes. Many handbooks cover the basic points of self-employment; some discuss the financial or legal implications in particular, others concentrate on small businesses in certain areas of activity. The purpose of this volume is to offer help in deciding what to read and where to turn for advice on specific categories of need; many recent publications are discussed and their merits noted. Readers of this volume will be those who are considering self-employment or setting up a small business, or those who have recently begun their own enterprise and need advice on how to develop from the initial stage. Large businesses or those who have been established for some time will still find value here as opportunities for training, improvement, development, relocation and so on can take place at any stage in the life of an enterprise, and many of the points noted in this book are relevant to business expansion as well as to initial start-up.

Professional advisers, especially careers advisers, will find useful the discussion of where information can be located, the names of various advisory and support bodies, and the data on educational and training opportunities. We also envisage that librarians will make use of this volume as a basis for evaluating the numerous titles available and deciding which might be the most appropriate in their situation.

The opening chapter – 'Education and training for small businesses' – stresses the vital importance of training in all aspects of a small enterprise, and the need to be aware of training requirements at every stage and at all levels of activity. Government schemes and initiatives are discussed, and information is given on courses available in further education colleges, in polytechnics and universities, and by open learning (correspondence, summer schools, workshops, etc.) specifically to improve the quality and success rate of new and developing enterprises.

The greater part of the book is devoted to the discussion of self-help guides, considered both as a general resource for advice and support, and as a specific help in certain stages of development; key areas of attention are the business plan, financial support, analysis of the market, premises, selling and distribution, publicity, advertising and record keeping. A follow-up chapter explores those guides aimed at particular trades and services.

Subsequent chapters look at reference materials that will help the small business, especially directories, at periodical publications to support activities, at the use of word processors and microcomputers in the small business context, and at the legal requirements that must be observed in starting up a new enterprise – particularly points relating to staffing and health and safety regulations.

The final chapter examines miscellaneous sources of advice and support; the key organizations here are the Small Firms Service and the Department of Trade and Industry, but very many more specialized schemes and specific organizations are mentioned that are relevant in certain situations.

It is inevitable in an area where interest is high and the rate of development is rapid that new publications will be constantly appearing, and that new editions of existing titles will be constantly issued; readers need always to seek out the most recent editions available to avoid relying on data that has been superseded by changes in law or regulations.

2

Education and training for small businesses

A disturbingly high percentage of new small businesses fail to survive for more than two years, and many more provide only the barest subsistence income to their proprietors. The Training Agency (formerly the Training Commission and before that the Manpower Services Commission) estimates that less than 20 per cent of new businesses have taken advantage of any management training, and the Agency is engaged in a campaign to increase awareness of facilities available, to adapt courses to firms' real requirements, provide financial inducements for participation and offer means of attendance or study patterns that are acceptable to hard-pressed people.

The activities of the Training Agency are multiplying and new areas of attack are regularly appearing; consequently, it is not possible to summarize all that is being done as new information is constantly being published. Readers must expect to use local careers libraries, Jobcentres and the Small Firms Service for the latest material on what is being offered and how.

The present official commitment to enterprise extends to all sectors of education; the Training Agency's 1988 initiative 'Enterprise in Higher Education' (EHE) offers up to £1 million to each university and polytechnic over a five-year period, and there has been a very positive response from these institutions. EHE is intended to encourage the growth of undergraduate courses

Setting up in Business

relevant to the attitudes and competencies needed in business, and promote a partnership between the employing community and the learning process. Part of the institutional enthusiasm can be attributed to the close connection between EHE requirements and the type of activities and courses that have been under development in higher education: discipline-based courses have been seen to be inadequate, and personal skills for employment are relevant both for small businesses and most other areas of work; teaching methods have been moving towards team work, contracts of learning, and broadening the teaching/learning base; pressures for institutional change have been mounting and EHE provides an additional impetus to achieve new directions; the opportunities to obtain private-sector finance have been increasingly attractive and EHE will further encourage this.

From the employer's or potential small business proprietor's viewpoint, relevance of courses will be increased by the contact between industry and the educational institutions, and by the wider base of skills offered; team work will be encouraged, students will work to budgetary and resource constraints and assessment will involve the employer as well as the institution.

To ensure that graduates get into the small business world at the end of their courses, the Department of Employment has launched several schemes including the Graduate Gateway Programme (GGP) which places graduates and other students into small firms for work experience, and the Graduate Enterprise Programme (GEP) which coordinates small-business training for recent graduates. Numbers of people involved in these schemes are growing very rapidly but from such a small base that overall national totals are still in hundreds rather than thousands. A recent leaflet from the Department of Employment, *Graduates: which door would you choose?* (1988), summarizes opportunities in small businesses, while a companion booklet, *Small firms: open your doors to graduates* (1988), explains to small firms what skills graduates can offer and how to recruit and train them successfully. Undergraduates can obtain information from institutional careers advisers, local careers libraries and from the booklet *Graduates in small businesses* issued by AGCAS, the Association of Graduate Careers Advisory Services. AGCAS also produce a Career Information Booklet *Self-employment and alternative work styles* which gives a range of options outside the conventional employment structure.

In this chapter we shall discuss, first, appropriate courses offered by educational establishments; secondly, the training facilities promoted by the Training Agency; and finally, other possibilities for training and education in this field.

COLLEGE-BASED COURSES

As we explained in the preceding section, the rate of change in the higher education sector is such that no book can attempt to give a full current picture of available facilities; individual university, polytechnic and college prospectuses will give details of their own provision and contact details for further information. Prospectuses can be found in careers libraries and public reference libraries; contact with a firm's local educational establishment should yield plenty of data on what is available. Colleges of Further Education offer a range of lower level courses, some of which may be aimed at particular qualifications such as BTEC awards (Business and Technical Education Council), Royal Society of Arts and City and Guilds of London Institute examinations: other courses will be run to meet likely demands without offering a paper qualification at the end.

Finding out what is on offer can be confusing; some printed guides have been issued, for example, the Scottish Education Department's *Education and training for small business* (SED/HMSO, 1986), and Colin Barrow's *Small business guide* (BBC Publications, rev. edn, 1984) gives a list in Section 8, 'Training', of some 300 colleges in the UK and the courses they offer relevant to the small business. The list gives details of types of course (short courses for setting up, longer courses, topic courses, consultancy, business clubs), and a contact name and telephone number; this has been an invaluable help but is now seriously out of date and does not reflect the growth that has taken place in recent years.

Undoubtedly the best means of discovering college-based provision is to use the database produced by PICKUP: Professional Industrial and Commercial Updating was launched by the Department of Education and Science in 1982 and covers England and Wales. (An allied programme, PICKUP Partnership Projects, operates in Scotland.) The programme aims to help colleges increase and improve their work in meeting the training, retraining and updating needs of employers and workforces; the nature of the training is specific, and its features are:

1. vocational priority;
2. for those in employment (rather than speculative courses for the jobless);
3. post-experience (rather than initial training);
4. collaborative – between colleges and employers;
5. short, part-time, flexible and cost-effective;
6. self-financing (the customer-consumer pays).

Emphasis is placed on tailor-made packages, action learning, independent study and on-site courses; a network of regional agents coordinate activity, and over 350 Local Collaborative Projects have been set up to bring employers and colleges together.

Details of PICKUP activities and the courses which underpin the programme can best be accessed through the Training Access Points (TAP) scheme; TAPs are databases of local educational provision coupled with three national databases, one of which is the PICKUP database. TAPs can be accessed through careers libraries, Jobcentres, many public libraries and further education centres; access can be online or via electronic mail, PRESTEL, on CD-ROM or microfiche.

Distance learning and open learning (working on material designed to be studied individually at home and in your own time, at your own pace, without the necessity of definite entrance criteria) have an obvious appeal to small businesses. Many polytechnics and universities are working together towards greater provision of material on this basis, and the Open University Open Business School runs a highly successful 'start up your own business course'. This is programmed to take 50 hours of student time over 9 months, and features workbooks, video and audio cassettes, and contact with an adviser; the culmination of the course is the presentation of a business plan to a panel of experts. Over 15,000 students have joined this course since 1983, and 20 per cent of the intake is from small firms. The Open College, the National Extension College, Henley Management College and the Institute of Marketing are all active in the field, and many other local colleges and consortia of educational establishments can be expected to offer similar open learning packages in the near future.

THE TRAINING AGENCY

The Training Agency is the principal channel for government initiatives and financial support; as these are developing constantly, it is essential to take care to find the latest information at the time of enquiry. The basic guide to services is the Department of Employment booklet *Action for jobs* which is re-issued at regular intervals and is widely available in Jobcentres, public libraries, schools and colleges. This includes brief details of all employment, training, enterprise and special needs programmes, and gives details of where to find further material on any aspect.

For the self-employed and small businesses, these programmes at present include several 'Training for Enterprise' schemes, described below, and details of the Small Firms Service, the Enterprise Allowance Scheme, Loan Guarantee Scheme and Business Expansion Scheme. Open learning and TAPs, mentioned earlier in this chapter, are also described in the booklet.

The Enterprise Allowance Scheme offers support to the unemployed who have been out of work for a minimum of eight weeks and who have a business venture in mind; currently £40 a week is payable for one year, and free advice is given by the Small Firms Service (whose services are fully described in Chapter 9). Applicants must be able to put £1000 into their business, probably by raising a loan or bank overdraft. Jobcentres carry full details of the EAS, which requires attendance at an initial self-employment awareness day to gain fundamental advice.

The Loan Guarantee Scheme helps new or existing small businesses to raise capital from financial institutions with a government guarantee in cases where lack of business experience might make support unlikely. The Business Expansion Scheme enables small firms to obtain support from private investors; an accountant would need to be consulted.

The main 'Training for Enterprise' programme aims to help those considering starting up in business and newly formed firms which require additional help to develop or expand. The Business Enterprise Programme (BEP) is the basic scheme for individuals about to start a business or who have just begun; Enterprise Allowance recipients will find it a suitable course. BEP is available free of charge and its objectives are to explore the viability of your ideas and consider its success; to understand the fundamental

Setting up in Business

principles of business administration and to prepare a detailed business plan. The programme is divided into a one-day Introductory Seminar and a main programme which covers six days, usually in three blocks of two days which may include weekends or evening within a four to five week total length. The topics covered in the main programme will usually include: personal resources, business structure, legal requirements, sources of finance, marketing, market research, pricing and product costing, sales forecasting, business planning, advertising and promotion, cash flow, time management, premises and capital equipment, profit and loss, books and record-keeping (tax, VAT and using an accountant), selling and negotiation skills, insurance requirements, action planning. The Graduate Enterprise Programme offers similar training to recent graduates.

The New Enterprise Programme (NEP) is intended for people starting businesses with the potential for growth and recruitment of staff; it consists of a sixteen-week full-time course held at a school of business studies.

The Firmstart programme covers similar ground on a part-time, weekend and evening basis over about six months; once again, this is for those whose businesses have the potential to offer employment eventually to at least ten staff.

The Private Enterprise Programme (PEP) consists of a series of thirteen seminars covering business management skills; they are problem-centred, and participants should see them as an opportunity to examine identified difficulties in their firms. The target market is owners or managers in small companies seeking to consolidate or expand. A small fee is charged.

Existing firms wishing to grow but lacking management resources can use the Management Extension Programme and Graduate Gateway Programme to learn from the skills of experienced managers or recent graduates on a secondment basis, organized by educational establishments or training consultancies but at minimal cost to the host firms.

The Training Agency also offers occasional shorter 'small business courses' over eight weeks, and 'self-employment courses' that last one to two weeks. Workshops are also presented on the kit *Your business success* which seeks to help formulate a business plan and analyse training needs.

The Vocational Educational and Training (VET) Group of the

Education and training for small businesses

Training Agency offers particular help in the provision of training and development of management techniques; the Group offers 'Local Consultancy Grants' which give aid to obtain professional advice on training needs and training objectives; 'Local Training Grants' offer financial assistance to employers for new or additional training or to rectify skill deficiency in the local labour market. Other VET Group initiatives include management development demonstration projects, management training and development projects, and a scheme for managing company expansion. Training Agency material and leaflets can be obtained from local offices (often in telephone books under 'Manpower Services Commission' until the 1988 title changes become established); Jobcentres and careers libraries will have basic information on the fundamental schemes, and details of VET Group activities should be sought from area offices (addresses and telephone numbers are shown in Figure 2.1).

Another Training Agency component, the Careers and Occupational Information Centre (COIC), produce a very basic leaflet *Self-employment* (Job Outline no. 82) and a more expanded and attractive summary of opportunities in the 'working in' series: no. 87 *Self-employment*.

OTHER TRAINING FACILITIES

Although the Training Agency and colleges provide the bulk of educational and training courses for small businesses, a variety of other providers have specific items to offer. Local Enterprise Agencies often have a training role to assist those who approach them for help, and various specific business associations and professional groups may have introductory courses or development schemes; details of these organizations and how to locate them will be discussed more fully in Chapter 9.

Similarly there are many schemes for encouraging young people to set up in business, and an advisory and training role is normally included; these are also explored in Chapter 9.

Two notable national organizations are CoSIRA (Council for Small Industries in Rural Areas), now the Rural Development Commission, and Project Fullemploy. CoSIRA/RDC, offers technical and managerial advice, short and long courses and

Setting up in Business

LIST OF VET GROUP AREA OFFICES

LONDON REGION

London North	6th Floor, 19-29 Woburn Place, London WC1 0LU	01-837 1288
London East	3rd Floor, Cityside House, 40 Adler Street, London E1 1EW	01-377 1866
London West	Lyric House, 149 Hammersmith Road, Hammersmith, London W14 0QL	01-602 7227
London South	Skyline House, 200 Union Street, London SE1 0LX	01-928 0800
Inner London South	20 Albert Embankment, London SE1 7TJ	01-735 0711
Inner London North	236 Grays Inn Road, London WC1X 8HL	01-278 0363

EAST MIDLANDS & EASTERN

Derbyshire	4th Floor, St Peters House, Gower Street, Derby DE1 1SB	0332 290550
Leicestershire & Northamptonshire	1st Floor, Rutland Centre, Halford Street, Leicester LE1 1TQ	0533 538616
Lincolnshire	5th Floor, Wigford House, Brayford Wharf, Lincoln LN5 7AY	0522 32266
Nottinghamshire	4th Floor, Lambert House, Talbot Street, Nottingham NG1 7FF	0602 413313
Bedfordshire & Cambridgeshire	Ground Floor, Wesley House, 19 Chapel Street, Luton LU1 2SE	0582 412828
Norfolk & Suffolk	Crown House, Crown Street, Ipswich, Suffolk IP1 3HS	0473 218951

WEST MIDLANDS

Birmingham & Solihull	15th & 16th Floors, Metropolitan House, 1 Hagley Road, Birmingham B16 8TG	021-456 1199
Coventry & Warwickshire	5th & 6th Floors, Bankfield House, 163 New Union Street, Coventry CV1 2PE	0203 631133
Dudley & Sandwell	6th Floor, Falcon House, The Minories, Dudley DY2 8PG	0384 455391
Staffordshire	Moorlands House, 24 Trinity Street, Hanley, Stoke on Trent ST1 5LN	0782 202733
The Marches Hereford/Worcester	2nd Floor, Hazledene House, Central Square, Telford, Shropshire TF3 4JJ	0952 507474
Wolverhampton & Walsall	2nd Floor, Jobcentre, 30 Market Street, Wolverhampton WV1 3AF	0902 311111

NORTHERN REGION

Cleveland	Corporation House, 73 Albert Road, Middlesbrough, Cleveland TS1 2RU	0642 241144
County Durham	Valley Street North, Darlington, Co Durham DL1 1TJ	0325 51146
Northumberland North Tynesdie & Newcastle	1st Floor, Broadacre House, Market Street, Newcastle-upon-Tyne NE1 6HH	091-232 6181
Sunderland, South Tyneside & Gateshead	Derwent House, Washington New Town, Tyne and Wear NE38 7ST	091-416 6161

NORTH WEST REGION

Bolton, Bury, Rochdale & Wigan	3rd Floor, Provincial House, Nelson Square, Bolton BL1 1PN	0204 397350
Cheshire	1st Floor, Spencer House, Dewhurst Road, Birchwood Centre, Warrington WA3 7PP	0925 826515
Cumbria	Thurlmere Building, 50 Lakes Road, Derwent Howe, Workington CA14 3YP	0900 66991
Lancashire	2nd, 3rd & 4th Floors, Duchy House, 96 Lancaster Road, Preston PR1 1HE	0772 59393
Merseyside Inner	4th Floor, Sefton House, Exchange Street East, Liverpool L2 3XR	051-236 0026
Merseyside Outer	7th Floor, Sefton House, Exchange Street East, Liverpool L2 3XR	051-236 0026
Manchester, Salford & Trafford	4th & 5th Floors, Boulton House, 17-21 Chorlton Street, Manchester M1 3HY	061-236 7222
Oldham, Tameside & Stockport	1st Floor, 1 St Peter's Square, Stockport SK1 1NN	061-477 8830

SCOTLAND

Ayrshire, Dumfries & Galloway	25 Bank Street, Kilmarnock KA1 1ER	0563 44044
Central and Fife	5 Kirk Loan, Corstophine, Edinburgh EH12 7HD	031-334 9821
Glasgow City	George House, 4th Floor, 36 North Hanover Street, Glasgow G1 2AD	041-552 3411
Grampian & Tayside	4th & 5th Floors, Argyll House, Marketgait, Dundee DD1 1UD	0382 29971
Highlands & Islands	3rd Floor, Metropolitan House, 31-33 High Street, Inverness IV1 1TX	0463 220555
Lanarkshire	Scomagg House, Crosshill Street, Motherwell ML1 1RU	0698 51411
Lothian & Borders	2-3 Queen Street, Edinburgh EH2 1JS	031-225 1377
Renfrewshire, Dumbarton and Argyll	5 Elm Bank Gardens, Charing Cross, Glasgow G2 4PN	041-226 554

SOUTH EAST REGION

Berkshire & Oxfordshire	5th Floor, Kings Point, 120 Kings Road, Reading, Berks. RG1 3DA	0734 586262
Buckinghamshire and Hertfordshire	2nd Floor, 31 Octagon Parade, High Wycombe, Bucks HP11 2LD	0494 33473
Essex	Globe House, New Street, Chelmsford, Essex CM1 1UG	0245 358548
Hampshire & Isle of Wight	25 Thackray Mall, Fareham Shopping Centre, Fareham, Hants PO16 0PQ	0329 285921
Kent	5th Floor, Mountbatten House, 28 Military Road, Chatham, Kent ME4 4JE	0634 44411
Surrey	Technology House, 48-54 Goldsmith Road, Woking, Surrey GU21 1LE	0486 228190
Sussex	Exchange House, Worthing Road, Horsham, West Sussex RH12 1SQ	0403 50244

SOUTH WEST REGION

Avon	PO Box 164, 4th Floor, Minster House, 27 Baldwin Street, Bristol BS99 7HR	0272 277116
Devon and Cornwall	6th Floor, Intercity House, Plymouth Station, Plymouth, Devon PL4 6AA	0752 671671
Dorset and Somerset	Crescent House, The Mount, Taunton, Somerset TA1 3TT	0823 259121
Gloucestershire and Wiltshire	Conway House, 33-35 Worcester Street, Gloucester GL1 3AJ	0452 24488

WALES

Dyfed & West Glamorgan	3rd Floor, Orchard House, Orchard Street, Swansea SA1 5AP	0792 460355
Gwent	Government Building, Cardiff Road, Newport, Gwent NP9 1YE	0633 56161
Gwynedd, Clwyd & Powys	Wynnstay Block, Hightown Barracks, Kingsmill Road, Wrexham LL13 8BH	0978 290333
Mid and South Glamorgan	5th Floor, Phase One Building, Ty Glas Road, Llanishen, Cardiff CF4 5PJ	0222 755744

YORKSHIRE AND HUMBERSIDE REGION

Wakefield, Doncaster and Barnsley	York House, 31-36 York Place, Leeds LS1 2EB	0532 450502
Bradford, Calderdale and Kirklees	Jubilee House, 33-41 Park Place, Leeds LS1 2RL	0532 446299
Humberside	4th Floor, Essex House, Manor House, Hull HU1 1YA	0482 226491
North Yorkshire and Leeds	Fairfax House, Merrion Street, Leeds LS2 8LH	0532 446181
Sheffield and Rotherham	8th Floor, Sheaf House, The Pennine Centre, Hawley Street, Sheffield S1 3GA	0742 701911

During the life of this publication local addresses may change.
JULY 1987

Figure 2.1   List of VET Group area offices

Education and training for small businesses

financial support to those intending to set up in rural areas or towns with fewer than 10,000 inhabitants. (Details of CoSIRA/RDC courses can be obtained from 141 Castle St, Salisbury, Wiltshire SP1 3TP, telephone 0722 336255, and from Rural Development Commission county offices.) Project Fullemploy provides training facilities and advice on self-employment principally to minority ethnic communities; there are six centres and details are available from the Central Office, 102 Park Village East, London NW1P 3SP, telephone 01-387-1222.

Overseas training and educational opportunities in foreign colleges and universities may be relevant in specific employment fields or for particular industries; specialized advice should be sought from professional bodies or employer groups in the relevant subject areas. Colin Barrow's *Small business guide* (BBC Publications, rev. edn, 1984) offers a list of universities and colleges with small business expertise.

For those interested in forming a cooperative, COIC publish *Worker co-operatives* (Job Outline no. 61), a pamphlet outlining the major points, listing organizations that could offer advice and assistance, and giving details of the two colleges that offer relevant courses (Beechwood College, Leeds, and the Cooperative College, Loughborough).

Michel Syrett and Chris Dunn's *Starting a business on a shoestring* (Penguin Books, 1988) provides useful coverage of education and training aspects of small businesses; a section of Chapter 3 entitled 'Where to study and train' gives brief details of colleges and other bodies offering courses. Appendix 4 discusses sources of 'small-business training', and Appendix 5 offers further ideas for young people.

In Chapter 9 of this volume, we shall mention other organizations and sources of advice, assistance and support for small businesses and the self-employed. It should be remembered that educational facilities and training form a part of the role of such organizations.

3

Self-help guides

GENERAL WORKS ON STARTING UP AND RUNNING A SMALL BUSINESS

This is a field of publishing that really seems to have taken off in the last few years, with new titles appearing every month. They all cover similar ground: getting an idea, testing the market, raising the money, finding premises, marketing and selling, doing the accounts, dealing with taxation, and employing people. However, there seem to be two broad approaches; some books help you to review, analyse and evaluate, while others offer direct practical help with procedures. Both are necessary. It is worth scanning a number of guides, therefore, to decide which seem to be the most appropriate.

Comprehensiveness and reliability are important, and the banks and national newspapers lend their names to some well-established and thorough texts. *The Guardian guide to running a small business*, edited by Clive Woodcock (Kogan Page, 7th edn, 1988) is due for publication at the time of writing (September 1988) and is fully updated to include 1988 Budget changes. The 6th edition (1987) gives very detailed information and advice under headings: The first steps; Getting organised; Sources of finance; Marketing; Planning the office; Benefiting from the tax system; Employing people; Choosing a computer; Health and safety; Business premises. It also has a short but highly relevant section giving addresses of helpful organizations. It is not a how-to-do-it manual, however, but an overview of the issues, possibilities and problems involved. *How to set up and run your own business* (Telegraph Publications, 6th edn, 1987) looks at premises, marketing and sales, and administration, but concentrates mainly on the financial aspects of running, controlling and developing the business. Godfrey Golzen's *Working for yourself: the Daily Telegraph guide to self-employment* (Kogan Page, 9th edn, 1987) has a slightly different slant, which is to outline opportunities. Part 1 covers the practicalities of running your own business, Part 2 lists businesses requiring capital, Part 3 is a directory of part-time opportunities requiring little initial cash investment, and Part 4 looks at freelance work. The *Lloyds Bank small business guide* by Sara Williams (Penguin, 1987) talks the prospective business owner through the various stages of starting up in a very detailed, practical, step-by-step fashion which is excellent for someone with little or no previous business experience; the book is highly recommended on this account. Chapter headings and vocabulary reflect the approach: Before taking the plunge; Getting a head start; How to sell your product; The working environment; Financial preparation and control; Tax; Planning for retirement. Specialized terminology is explained, and the book is packed with checklists, summaries and examples at every stage. Not as detailed but equally approachable and realistic is *The greatest little business book: the essential guide to starting a small business*, by Peter Hingston (Auchterarder: Hingston, rev. edn, 1987). It is particularly useful for all the worked examples supplied. Inadequate on their own, but valuable as brief basic introductory works containing referrals to other appropriate agencies, are Maurice Anslow's *Working for yourself* (Ward Lock, 1987) and *Starting your own business*, edited by Edith Rudinger (Consumers' Association/Hodder & Stoughton, rev. edn, 1987).

Important aspects of starting a small business are (a) finding out whether you are the right sort of person to be self-employed, and (b) doing adequate forward planning realistically to assess the potential of the idea. *Be your own boss kit*, by D. S. Watkins *et al.* (National Extension College, 1982) is well supplied with checklists, summaries and questionnaires designed to test the person and the business idea. The authors stress that effective use of the kit involves 'really *working* at answering the questions we raise explicitly in each section ... "Checkpoint" sections are scattered throughout the *Kit* which we hope will encourage you to stop and think about what you have just read, and apply the advice and information to your own situation'. This is the aim of all the guides – to encourage honest self-analysis and check idealistic visions. Thus the emphasis in *Starting a successful small business*, by M. J. Morris (Kogan Page, 1985) is on preparation and detailed forward planning. The *Lloyds Bank small business guide* (Penguin, 1987), already discussed in this section, starts by looking at 'you and your ideas', with questions which enable the reader to begin some self-analysis. Evaluating the possibilities is the subject of Stephen Halliday's *Which business? how to select the right opportunity for starting up* (Kogan Page, 1987). Assessing yourself and your idea are covered very thoroughly and very effectively with the help of case studies and lists of questions and considerations in *Starting a business on a shoestring*, by Michel Syrett and Chris Dunn (Penguin, 1988), which offers basic advice on other aspects of starting a business. More general reading can be found in *The freelance alternative*, by Marianne Gray (Piatkus, 1987). Subtitled 'for people who want freedom, challenge or independence in their lives', it encourages the reader to think about alternatives and possibilities, and is aimed at those perhaps at some turning point in their lives. A rather arbitrary list of contacts is provided with no information as to the purpose of each.

'Women and children' are not forgotten in these start-up guides. Deborah Fowler provides all the basic information in *The woman's guide to starting your own business* (Grapevine, 1988) but in addition examines the particular issues women might have to face because of the family situation, tax implications, and so on. *How to be a successful business woman: working for yourself*, by Janet W. MacDonald (Methuen, 1987) is very general and is based on the author's definition of 'successful' which is that 'you are making more money than you would by putting the same amount of time and effort into working for someone else'. In addition to the sources of information for young people in business mentioned in Chapter 9, a useful publication is *Want to be your own boss?* by Nic Davies (Royal Jubilee Trusts, 1986). It is an introductory guide offering 'first-step pointers to resources, advice and guidance for young people hoping to set up a business on their own'.

Other useful general titles worth looking at are *Starting a business: a practical handbook with examples*, Richard Hargreaves

Self-help guides

(Heinemann, 2nd edn, 1987) which is very thorough and useful for its examples of official forms; *Getting started: how to set up your own business* (Kogan Page, 1988); *How to start and run your own business*, by Mike Mogano (Graham & Trotman, 6th edn, 1988); *The small business action kit*, John Rosthorn *et al.* (Kogan Page, 2nd edn, 1988) which contains checklists, worksheets, flowcharts and summaries designed to help the beginner cope with the essentials. *The complete entrepreneur: a guide to survival for the small business*, David Oates (Mercury, 1987) is good background reading. It uses case studies to draw out advice and conclusions about single-skill enterprises, franchising and cooperatives, ways to raise capital and to reduce the red tape.

It can be stimulating to read case studies alongside the practical guides. *Small firms in action: case histories in entrepreneurship*, by Peter M. Chisnall (McGraw Hill, 1987) examines enterprises helped by New Enterprises Programmes at Manchester Business School with MSC support. *Small business breakthrough*, John Blake *et al.* (Blackwell, 1985) presents case studies of eleven small companies, winners of a business competition sponsored by industry and local authorities, and follows their fortunes. The cases draw attention to broader issues such as the need for originality and for excellence in finance and marketing strategies. *Winners*, by Robert Bruce (Sidgwick & Jackson, 1986) is another set of case studies based on the winners of the Industrial Achievement Award. Small businesses may become big business, or at least can learn from it, and a potentially 'good read' for the small businessman is *The winning streak*, by Walter Goldsmith and David Clutterbuck (Weidenfeld & Nicolson, 1984), an analysis of Britain's outstanding companies. The book is arranged under headings such as leadership, market orientation and innovation, and concludes that there are 'eight major perceptions' shared by the successful companies which influence their behaviour and thereby their profitability. It might be worth working on sharing those perceptions!

HOME-BASED AND PART-TIME OPPORTUNITIES

For various reasons, many people need to work from home or to supplement their existing income by additional part-time work. A useful book in this category for sparking off ideas is a *Which?*

publication *Earning money at home: how to brush up a skill or hobby to money-making standards*, edited by Edith Rudinger (Hodder & Stoughton/Consumers' Association, rev. edn, 1986). Practical issues such as planning the initiative with the family, insurance, costing, selling, and keeping accounts are dealt with briefly. A vast range of practical, intellectual and service jobs are then examined, grouped according to whether they use previous job experience, existing skills, craftwork, or are new ventures. There is not a lot of information on any one topic but it is a good starting point and the general advice on starting up is helpful. *Working from home: 201 ways to earn money* by Marianne Gray (Piatkus, 1982) is similarly organized: it examines general practical and legal issues, then outlines the requirements of a range of specific jobs and services. There are 20 pages of 'contacts': addresses of general and specialized agencies and professional associations, with information on courses, training and further reading. More ideas can be found in *The home-earner: the complete guide to money-making ideas from home*, Christine Brady (Corgi, 1987), and *Making money part time: a practical guide to ways of earning extra income*, Alan and Deborah Fowler (Sphere, 1986). The implications of using home as a business base are particularly well covered in Malcolm Bird's *Daily Mail guide to working from home* (Associated Magazines, 1987) and *Running a business from home*, by Alan Terry (Sphere, 1985).

COOPERATIVES AND FRANCHISES

Members of a cooperative all share in its control, own the assets or are aiming to do so, and are all either workers or founder members with equal voting rights. Setting up is adequately described in *Worker cooperatives* (COIC, n.d.) and John Pearce's *Running your own cooperative* (Kogan Page, 1984), both of which are discussed in Chapter 9 under the heading 'Support for Cooperatives'. Additional new material can be found in *How to start and run your own business*, Mike Mogano (Graham & Trotman, rev. edn, 1988), a practical handbook on starting up a new business. *The complete entrepreneur: a guide to survival for the small business*, David Oates (Mercury, 1987) uses case studies to illustrate the guidelines it offers. The best source of information on the setting

Self-help guides

up and operation of cooperatives is the Cooperative Development Agency (CDA) at Broadmead House, 21 Panton Street, London SW1Y 4DR (telephone 01-839-2988). As well as advice and documentation, it can supply addresses of local cooperative development agencies. Other sources are examined in *Starting your own business*, edited by Edith Rudinger (Consumers' Association/Hodder & Stoughton, rev. edn, 1987) mentioned elsewhere in this book. The *Lloyds Bank small business guide* (Penguin, 1987) also has a brief section mainly on the legal aspects of forming a cooperative.

Most of the general self-help guides contain some information on franchising, a system whereby, at its best, a business is set up and thoroughly established in all its aspects, and franchises based on the pilot model are then sold to suitable people who develop their own business on their own territory, but with full back-up and support from the franchisor. There is a particularly good section on franchises in the *Lloyds Bank small business guide* (Penguin, 1987) where Sara Williams explains the nature of franchising very fully and effectively, and examines the legal and financial implications. The would-be franchisee should certainly consult *Franchising*, by Peter Hall and Rob Dixon (Pitman, 1988), an excellent explanatory handbook which also offers guidelines for the prospective franchisor. *The successful franchise: a working strategy*, Golden Square Services Ltd (Gower, 1985) is a practical step-by-step manual for evaluating, choosing and operating a franchise. *Taking up a franchise*, by Colin Barrow and Godfrey Golzen (Kogan Page, 4th edn, 1987) is a fully detailed guide with explanations and advice on all stages of the operation, and includes a directory of current franchising opportunities. However, the book is packed with franchise company adverts, which may stimulate ideas in the reader but which make the overall appearance of the content rather confusing. *The good franchise guide*, by Tony Attwood and Len Hough (Kogan Page, 1988) is 'an independent survey of over 400 franchises in the UK', and reviews those currently on the market at less than £250,000. Each is examined against a formula layout, with comments, and the work is indexed to allow the reader to approach by cost, type of franchise, ranking and name. This is a work that will need to be kept thoroughly up to date to be of use but can be supplemented by current information in *The Franchise Magazine* (see the section on periodicals in Chapter 6), though this may be less objective.

SPECIFIC ASPECTS OF STARTING AND RUNNING A SMALL BUSINESS

The general self-help guides between them contain information and advice on all aspects of starting and running a small business and becoming self-employed, but many of those topics will need to be studied in greater depth and detail once the first step has been taken. There are plenty of books on the market to help, and as far as possible those examined in this section are aimed specifically at people in small businesses as they have the right approach to scale and economy.

The business plan

Drawing up a business plan is an essential, and certainly a useful, starting point in setting up a business on even the smallest scale. It helps the individual clarify his or her ideas, and if loans or grants are to be applied for, it assists the financier in assessing both the idea and the professionalism and commitment of the client. The case for a business plan and strategies for constructing it are clearly and effectively presented in a videotape currently obtainable at a nominal cost from the Midland Bank: *Helping you succeed in business* (Midland, 1987; 25 minutes). It ties in with a booklet (one of a series) from the Midland called *The business plan*, and looks in turn at the business background, products and services, assessment of market, and financial considerations. The video format is effectively used with short dramatic sketches to illustrate the points made; the emphasis is on encouraging planning and a professional approach. The National Westminster Bank has produced a series of books called the NatWest Small Business Bookshelf, one of which is called *A business plan* (Pitman, 1988). It is thorough and detailed, with summaries, worked examples and checklists. The section on preparing a business plan in *The greatest little business book*, by Peter Hingston (Auchterarder: Hingston, rev. edn, 1987) offers descriptions and explanations, a format or model to build on which takes into account all possibilities from which the user can select what is relevant, layout suggestions, and a full worked example which is particularly useful. Richard Hargreaves in *Starting a business* (Heinemann, 2nd edn, 1987) offers detailed and well-presented information, and there is a substantial chapter on writing a business plan in *Starting a business on a*

Self-help guides

shoestring, Michel Syrett and Chris Dunn (Penguin, 1988), which throughout is a clearly expressed, jargon-free text. For those who have never seen a business plan, however, the lengthy narrative approach could be daunting, and Peter Hingston's examples really allow the reader to see how it can look in practice. The source of information for the true business plan enthusiast is *The business plan workbook*, Colin Barrow (Kogan Page, 1988). It is a series of 24 assignments based on the content of a business course at Cranfield Institute of Technology. Each business plan is divided into phases, with worksheets and reading matter accompanying each phase. It is not really aimed at the beginner or home-based spare-time worker.

Financial support

Where money is to be borrowed, approaching the main banks (eg, Lloyds, National Westminster, Midland and Barclays) and the appropriate government departments (eg, Department of Employment Small Firms Service and Department of Trade and Industry) for their introductory booklet on loans, grants and other sources of finance, is a useful first step. Practical introductory works are *Raising finance: the Guardian guide for the small business*, Clive Woodcock (Kogan Page, 2nd edn, 1985) which is out of date in some of the detail but is very sound, and Peter Ibbetson's *How to raise business finance* (Plymouth: Northcote House, 1987). One of the Allied Dunbar Money Guides, *Running your own business*, by David Williams (Longman, 1988), looks at all the financial aspects of starting up and maintaining the business: raising capital, borrowing, financial planning, minimizing tax, credit and marketing, and so on. Useful for reference are *Maximising opportunities under the BES*, Patrick Way (Longman, 1987), and the *Arthur Young guide to financing for growth: ten alternatives for raising capital*, by Robert Owen et al. (Wiley, 1986). The first examines investment opportunities and tax incentives resulting from the Finance Act 1983 and the Business Expansion Scheme (BES). It contains specimens of the necessary legal forms. The second is a more general overview of financing small businesses.

Finding the market

Researching the potential market is an essential step in the start-up process. A useful general work aimed at, among others, managers of small businesses, is *Do your own market research*, by Paul N. Hague and Peter Jackson (Kogan Page, 1987). It is a practical guide to deciding whether market research is necessary (although stronger clearer guidelines are needed here), how to set objectives, do field and desk research, and how to carry out sampling questionnaire design, interviewing of all kinds, group discussions, clinics, surveys, data analysis and presentation of findings. Targeted at a more specific audience is *Successful marketing for the small business: the Daily Telegraph guide*, Dave Patten (Kogan Page, 2nd edn, 1988). The new edition is brought thoroughly up to date in examining all aspects of selling, researching and marketing, and offers plenty of practical advice as does Derek Waterworth's *Marketing for the small business* (Macmillan Education, 1987).

Location and premises

Most of the material on preparing a business plan stresses the importance of choosing the correct location and appropriate premises. This is the subject of two specialized guides. *How to choose the right business premises*, by Keith Jones (Telegraph Publications, 1988) is not aimed solely at the small business, but is potentially useful in its coverage of leasing and buying commercial properties including shops, offices, factories, hotels and catering establishments. It summarizes the legal implications and offers advice on all aspects of the move including the possibility of obtaining grants. *How to choose business premises: a guide for the small firm*, Howard Green et al. (Kogan Page, 1986) lists useful addresses and Areas of Government Assistance. It is very thorough and covers topics such as the implications of working from home; assessing the location, image and convenience of premises; building and health law and regulations; leases and insurance; moving premises and how to publicize it; designing, organizing and converting work spaces. There are informative case studies. The health and safety considerations relating to premises and equipment are nowhere better expressed than in *Essentials of health and safety at work*, Health & Safety Executive (HMSO, 1988). Described on the front cover as 'excellent help for smaller firms', it is a large-format paperback with clear illustrations and diagrams.

Colour-coded sections set out in brief and effective form how to plan for safety, and how to handle potentially dangerous activities and materials such as electricity, fire, and handling and storing dangerous substances.

Buying, selling and distribution

A number of Kogan Page publications cover buying, selling and distribution in the small business. *Buying for business: how to get the best deal from your suppliers*, Tony Attwood (Kogan Page, 1988) is directed at the small business, and advises on assessing needs, different types of contract, buying a service, and financing your purchases. *Importing for the small business: the Daily Telegraph guide*, Mag Morris (Kogan Page, 2nd edn, 1988) and its companion *Export for the small business*, Henry Deschampsneufs (Kogan Page, 1984) are complete guides to the export and import processes, and examine in detail the specialized documentation, payment arrangements, legal requirements and procedures involved. Both contain specimen documents. *Importing* is fully updated and includes EEC changes introduced in January 1988. *Distribution for the small business*, Nicholas Mohr (Kogan Page, 1988) is an inexpensive paperback reviewing the advantages of various distribution and despatch methods from motorbike messengers to roll-on/roll-off containers.

Production management

Manufacturing and production seems to be covered mainly by books on specific trades, or else in general management texts. However there is one current work available aimed specifically at small firms. It is *Small business: production operations management*, by Terry Hill (Macmillan, 1987) in the Macmillan Small Business series.

Publicity and advertising

One of the most difficult tasks for the person running a small business, particularly for the sole trader, perhaps working from home and providing a service rather than a product, is getting known. *Effective advertising: the Daily Telegraph guide for the small business*, H. C. Carter (Kogan Page, 1986) is a realistic guide for even the smallest of businesses. It advises on how to decide why, when and where to advertise, how to write it and present it, and on the use of agents and consultants. All outlets are covered: press, cinema, radio and TV, direct mail order, outdoor and transport advertising, and so on. Advertising is essential but may have to be a low priority financially for the beginner when measured against other necessary costs like basic equipment and premises. Jim Dudley outlines many relatively inexpensive ways of creating an image and getting you and the business known through advertising, sales promotion and public relations in his book *How to promote your own business: a guide to low budget publicity* (Kogan Page, 1988). *The secrets of successful low-budget advertising*, Patrick Quinn (Heinemann, 1987) is about 'advertising on a shoe-string' and is directed at the small business. There is discussion of all aspects of writing, artwork, strategy and outlets, with practical examples. The book is written in a punchy style that will appeal to some readers and alienate others, but the visual examples are very good. *The secrets of successful copywriting* by the same author (Heinemann, 1986) is written for the full-time copywriter, and is not a basic work, but is full of useful ideas for anyone who has time to study it.

Writing business documents

Advertising is part of the broader communications process generated by running a small business, and the trader may be involved in writing all his or her own business documents and letters. In writing letters, a few standard formats will be necessary for regular correspondence, and there are two books which offer models for most business situations (which can in any case be modified to suit individual needs). *Readymade business letters*, Jim Dening (Kogan Page, 1986) offers useful specimens, but is particularly helpful for its advice on how and when to use different types of letter, when to use a particular tone of voice, and who to send change-of-address and other documents to. It is a guide to usage as well as wording. *Instant business letters*, Mary Bosticco (Gower, 2nd edn, 1985) is arranged by type of procedure (credit and collection, adjustments and complaints, and so on) and consists of numbered paragraphs which can be combined at will to

Self-help guides

achieve the desired letter. It is suggested that the whole book can be passed to a typist, with the numbers of the appropriate paragraphs written on a piece of paper. It is an exhaustive sourcebook for forms of words and can easily be adapted for less standard letters. It includes advice and information on the appearance of documents: devising a house style, choosing stationery, and so on, and on correctness: forms of address, punctuation and other grammatical matters. These points are developed in *The business writing workbook: a guide to defensive writing skills*, Ian Stewart (Kogan Page, 1987). There are exercises to help you develop and use concise vocabulary, correct punctuation and grammar, and satisfactory sentences and paragraphs. A range of written documents is covered: memos, letters, reports, office stationery, forms and manuals, meetings documentation, curriculum vitae and applications.

Book-keeping and accounts

Financial administration is for many small business people the tiresome chore at the end of the week or month, particularly onerous if they work alone. Basic financial records are a priority, however, and to identify an appropriate system and apply it from day one, rather than letting something evolve (or not!) is essential. *Simple cash books for small businesses*, Paul Ordidge (Kogan Page, 1986) is very basic, very thorough and very clear. Practical guidance is given on recording cash and cheque payments and income, controlling expenditure, reconciling cash books with bank statements, using pre-printed cash books, and VAT. Some specific problems are highlighted, and there are recommended readings. More complex and advanced is A. G. Piper's *Book-keeping* (Hodder & Stoughton, 1984) in the Teach Yourself series. It includes preparing and adjusting accounts and the balance sheet, and looks at the implications of partnerships, depreciation and so on. The tiny home-based business would not need to use most of this, for others it is an excellent introduction. *Principles of book-keeping and accounts*, J. Paul (Primrose Publishers, 1988) is broader in scope again, and is directed at students and small-business owners. It is clear and explanatory. For those needing knowledge of the full range of procedures involved in accountancy, *Accounting made simple*, Wilfred Hingley (Heinemann, rev. edn, 1988) is a good introduction as it is prepared as a basis for foundation or intermediate stages of the professional accountancy examinations and for BTEC courses. Most of the small business self-help guides stress the importance of having an accountant, however, and books on accounting (rather than basic book-keeping) should be used as a method of gaining insight into your accountant's requirements rather than of becoming an amateur accountant.

Non-payment will almost inevitably be a significant financial problem for a small business. A concise and lively little Department of Employment booklet is a good first read. It is *Prompt payment please: a guide for suppliers and buyers*, Central Office of Information for Department of Employment (HMSO, rev. edn, 1988) and its aim is to 'encourage healthy cash flow management'. It emphasizes the need for suppliers and buyers to have a 'clear and consistent policy on payment' and to seek fuller advice on credit management, factoring and legal action. It gives practical advice and information plus lists of further reading and helpful organizations. A more substantial volume is *A guide to successful debt collecting*, by Andrew Theumissen (Rose-Jordan, 1982). It is a very practical step-by-step guide for those who want or need to collect their own debts and do it successfully. There is advice on how to prevent debts occurring in the first place, and how to use solicitors and the courts when it becomes essential. There are specimen letters and court forms with checklists of steps and actions to be taken. There is also *Debt collecting made easy*, Peter Buckland (Kogan Page, 1987) with similar information. Broader in scope is *Business rip-offs and how to avoid them*, Tony Attwood (Kogan Page, 1987), which aims to help readers identify situations where they are being ripped off, defrauded or simply faced with incompetence. Case studies based on real events are used as a way of presenting problems and step-by-step guidance on how to handle them assertively, legally and effectively. There is an outline of county court procedure and a good further reading list.

4

Opportunities in specific trades and services

For those who still have not made up their minds, a number of books exist which review a range of activities. Rosemary Pettit's *Occupation, self-employed* (Wildwood, 1981) gives a descriptive outline of jobs arranged under broad general headings: plants and animals; paper and pictures; shops and selling; house and home; children and teaching; crafts and manufactures; eating and entertaining. There is an appendix of factual information on courses, finance and information and advice services. Though becoming out of date in some of the detail, *Small beginnings*, by Alan Bollard (Intermediate Technology Publications, 1984) is a useful examination of small business opportunities in brewing, printing, recycling, small repair and service garages, small-scale cheese production and the brick, wool textile and plastic industries. *Starting from scratch: 50 profitable business opportunities*, Joe Sutherland Gould (Wiley, 1987) is American, so the financial figures and some other data are inappropriate, but otherwise the book gives a brief and honest overview of 50 possible businesses, all relevant in the UK.

There is a vast range of books available on how to acquire and run specific types of small business, usually written by people who have had experience in the business. The publishers Kogan Page have a series called Working for Yourself. Titles available include: *Running your own catering business* (1984), . . . *winebar* (1984), . . .

building business (1985), ... *hairdressing salon* (1986), *Working for yourself in the arts and crafts* (1986), *Running your own restaurant* (1986), ... *typing service* (1987), ... *small hotel* (rev. edn, 1988), and ... *estate agency* (1988). In each there is general information on starting and running a small business, then specific information on matters relevant to the business under discussion. In *Running your own restaurant*, for example, there is information and advice on food and drink, kitchen equipment, restaurant furnishings and equipment, and the daily operation, followed by excellent lists of further reading and useful addresses. Other publishers have similar series covering occupations ranging from sewing and knitting at home to running your own boarding kennels. David & Charles Business Books currently include *Making and managing a photographic studio* (1982), ... *a smallholding* (1986), ... *an antique shop* (1986), ... *an art and craft shop* (2nd edn, 1986), ... *a public house* (2nd rev. edn, 1986), *Selling crafts* (1986), and *Doing bed and breakfast* (1987). They are basic but helpful. For example, the bed and breakfast guide covers satisfactorily in 96 pages effective advertising, finance and insurance, fire regulations and precautions, health and hygiene, furnishing and equipment, seasonal and year-round work, charging, and The Breakfast (with menus). There are appendices covering minimum standards, useful addresses, fire rules and the content of a typical insurance policy.

Retailing is an area currently well provided for by the publishers. *The retail handbook: a practical guide to running a successful small retail business*, by Ann Foster and Bill Thomas (McGraw Hill, 1981) concentrates on the essentials: staff, money, stock, legal considerations and the rights and responsibilities of retailers. Also potentially helpful and perhaps more attractively written and presented, is *How to start and run your own shop*, P. Levene (Graham & Trotman, 2nd edn, 1988). *Buying a shop: the Daily Telegraph guide*, A. St J. Price (Kogan Page, 3rd edn, 1986) also covers the essentials in a clear and informative manner.

Small-scale cooking is the subject of books such as *Cook for hire*, Michelle Berriedale-Johnson (Macdonald, 1987) and *Cooking for cash*, Jennifer Curry (David & Charles, 1983). The latter is a realistic introduction to small-scale catering from home, illustrated with case studies. At the other end of the scale, *Thinking of buying a restaurant*, by Colin C. English (David & Charles, 1983) concentrates on the business and administrative aspects of the job

Opportunities in specific trades and services

rather than on food and drink. It is very thorough and detailed in its coverage, down to copyright requirements for the use of music in restaurants.

Books mentioned above are just a tiny sample of what is available. In almost every area of trade or service that an individual may want to try, almost certainly someone has been there before and written an anecdotal or practical book about the experience. Those currently available can best be traced by keyword in the monthly microfiche issues of *Whitaker's Books in print*, and the CD-ROM *Bookbank*.

5

Reference materials

Many of the self-help guides examined elsewhere in this book cover very thoroughly all aspects of starting a business, but not necessarily in great depth or detail as individual needs vary in practice and factual data rapidly becomes out of date. Reference works, in which facts, definitions and current information can be checked, are therefore essential, and the potential range of specialized material is enormous. From plumbing to second-hand bookselling there are subject dictionaries, directories, encyclopaedias and handbooks, and it would be inappropriate to try to list them all in a work of this scope – the public reference or commercial and technical library will be able to advise on what is available. The items cited in this chapter, therefore, are reference materials which underpin the process of setting up and running *any* business and additional material can be located in the section on legal requirements.

DICTIONARIES AND ENCYCLOPAEDIAS

Though many authors will assume their readers' familiarity with the vocabulary of their subject, unfamiliar terminology can be a problem for the person new to the business world. The *Penguin business dictionary*, Michael Greener (Viking Press, 1987) was first published in 1970 as the *Penguin dictionary of commerce* and is now in its third edition. It contains over 2500 definitions of words, phrases and business jargon, and is fully cross-referenced. There are helpful brief outlines of the relevant Acts. *The Economist pocket entrepreneur*, Colin Barrow (Blackwell/The Economist Publications, 1987) is an alphabetically arranged encyclopaedic dictionary that defines terms and jargon, and describes institutions, practices and concepts relevant to small businesses and entrepreneurship. The emphasis is on careful explanation. Encyclopaedic in scope, *The business fact finder*, edited by H. Johanssen (Kogan Page, 1987) covers every area of business administration: business organization, finance, property and premises, staffing, marketing and distribution, financial issues, and management. Each section is written by an expert in the field and provides essential basic facts on the topic plus a list of further sources of information. This work might be a good investment for the 'larger small business', because although it is subject to the usual problem of the finer details becoming out of date, the underlying principles will remain sound and it is a very reliable reference source. The updating problem is overcome in the loose-leaf encyclopaedias which can be regularly amended as significant new information becomes available. Useful in this context is *Croner's reference book for the self-employed and smaller business* (Croner, 1976; monthly amendments) which explains the law affecting those categories of people. Croner's services include a number of other loose-leaf works potentially useful to small businesses as reference tools. They are Croner's *Health and safety at work: an A-Z guide to health and safety regulations* (1979; 2-monthly amendments); *Buying and selling law: the law on buying and selling goods and services* (1982; 2-monthly amendments); *Management information manual* (1978; irregular amendments); *Reference book for VAT* (1973; monthly amendments).

DIRECTORIES AND HANDBOOKS

Directories are local, national or international listings of people, companies and organizations, products or services, and can be used to identify potential suppliers, customers, outlets and competition – and indeed, to draw attention to your own company once it is established. For the person starting up in business, local directories will probably be the most useful; national and international directories can be identified as required. The directory best known to most is the national telephone directory, now called *The phone book* (British Telecommunications plc), and its companion *Yellow pages*, both issued free to subscribers in the telephone area covered by the directories, and also available for purchase in hard-copy or microfiche formats. Larger public libraries will normally hold a complete set. The *Yellow pages* is arranged under headings by type of business and is a good guide to local firms in each telephone area. It is not exhaustive, as there is a mixture of paid and discretionary entries, but all the significant companies should be there. Covering much smaller areas, the *Thomson local directory* (Thomson Directories, annual) lists shops, services, suppliers and businesses under classified headings with a name index.

Other local information can be found in local authority directories, for example, the annual *City of Birmingham directory of industry and commerce* (Guardian Communications). The 1988 edition has a 200-page alphabetical listing of local firms, a classified section organized by trade or product, with an alphabetical subject index in four languages and an index to advertisers. Additionally, there are advertisements and announcements about business services in the area: start-ups, property services, support and so on. Chambers of Commerce produce membership lists and often also more wide-ranging and informative directories. Thus the 1987/88 edition of *The Merseyside, West Cheshire and North Wales directory of industry and commerce* (Guardian Communications, annual) contains some 60 pages of information about the Chambers involved, their officers and services, in addition to the usual directory format: an alphabetical list of companies in the region, and a classified section arranged by trade and product with an alphabetical subject index.

There are handbooks and compendia of information available that offer a broader and more coherent picture of business potential and industrial opportunities than can be deduced from the directories. The two examples described are no longer completely up to date but offer a useful starting point when the groundwork is being done. The *Industrial development guide 1986* compiled by Cambridge Information & Research Services Ltd (Longman, 8th edn, 1986) reviews industrial development incentives and prospects nationally and regionally, lists and describes the development

Reference materials

agencies, and has a substantial section devoted to county surveys, each with map, population and labour statistics, travel, transport and communications information, a statement about the county industrial policy, and names of local contacts. The *Business location handbook* for 1986/87 (Beacon Publications, 1986) is a 'complete guide to the selection of industrial and commercial property throughout the UK', outlining local conditions and contacts. There are sections on public and private sources of finance, enterprise zones, freeports, science/research parks, local authorities' services, distribution and communications networks, property and construction, and surveys and statistics. Though factual data would need to be checked against more up-to-date sources by the user when necessary, this volume offers practical information and, at the early stages of planning, a range of possibilities against which to measure a business idea.

The directories highlighted in this section are mostly very general and very local, but in the start-up process the individual is likely to need access to a wide range of contacts and points of referral. The self-help guides discussed in a separate chapter should therefore be looked at as very specialized mini-directories, as many of them list contact organizations appropriate to each stage of starting a business. The *Lloyds Bank small business guide*, Sara Williams (Penguin, 1987) is a good example as it has a chapter-by-chapter listing of organizations (and readings) appropriate to the topic under discussion.

6

Periodical publications

Periodicals, published as the name suggests at regular intervals, are one way of keeping up to date with news, new developments and initiatives, changes in the law and potential contacts. The central public library in towns and cities will normally carry a good range of national and local periodicals, bulletins and newsletters, and staff will willingly help users trace the small business titles some of which are examined here. *Small business digest* (1981–) is a quarterly publication issued by the National Westminster Bank Small Business Service. It contains brief practical articles on law, taxation and finance, and business administration. Contributors are not always employees of the NatWest, and coverage is national and quite general. Some of the relevant central government departments also produce periodicals with national coverage. The Department of Trade and Industry's *In business now* is a free newspaper issued every other month, subtitled 'News for growing businesses from the department for Enterprise'. It provides news of developing companies, information about awards and DTI services, and has a classified advertisement section. The emphasis is on encouragement and the stimulation of interest and activity in business. The Department of Employment Small Firms Service issues the Small Firms Factsheet at frequent intervals (for example, there were fourteen factsheets between January and mid-July 1988). Using press release format, they give news of initiatives, loans, awards, publications, useful organizations and contacts, health and

Periodical publications

safety at work information, and summaries of new law, budget statements and so on.

Many associations and institutions publish periodicals and newsletters which will probably be free to members or available in the commercial or reference sections of central public libraries. The Association of Independent Businesses specializes, among other things, in the operation of smaller firms and publishes *Independent business* monthly. For those interested particularly in mail order, direct mail and franchising, the Institute of Small Business has a collection of information and issues *New business ideas* (monthly). The same Institute, in association with Chartsearch Publications, produces the monthly *Business opportunities digest* which analyses over 20 business opportunities in each issue. The National Federation of Self Employed and Small Businesses (NFSE) specializes in information on methods of becoming self-employed, setting up in business and running small businesses. It provides information and news in its monthly publication *First voice*. The following list shows the main organizations and their publications relevant to small businesses:

Alliance of Small Firms & Self Employed People Ltd
279 Church Road, London SE19 2QQ. Tel: 01–653–7288
Business informer (q); *Business start-up package*.

Association of Independent Businesses
108 Weston Street, London SE1 3QB. Tel: 01–403–4066
Independent business (10 p.a.)

Institute of Small Business
57 Mortimer Street, London W1N 7TB. Tel: 01–637–4383
New business ideas (m); *Business opportunities digest* (m)

National Federation of Self Employed and Small Businesses (NFSE)
32 St Anne's Road West, Lytham St Annes, Lancs. FY8 1NY.
Tel: 0253 720911
First voice (m)

Small Business Bureau
32 Smith Square, London SW1P 3HH. Tel: 01–222–9000
Small business (m)

35

Setting up in Business

Teesside Small Business Club *and* National Forum of Small Business Clubs
52 Corporation Road, Middlesbrough, Cleveland TS1 2RN. Tel: 0642 223421

Teesside Small Business Club *Bulletin* (m); *Small Business Guides* (members only); Reports; List of members.

Local business news and information, potentially relevant even if not specifically concerned with *small* businesses, can be obtained through Chamber of Commerce journals, for example: *Westminster: the magazine of the Westminster Chamber of Trade* (m); *Trident: the monthly business magazine of the Merseyside Chambers of Trade*; *Midlands industry and commerce: the Birmingham and West Midlands Chambers of Commerce journal* (m). Each of these reflects developments, activities and potential within the local business environment. They contain articles ranging from the practical to the reflective, display advertising, and classified advertisements or trade indexes. There may be more specific local publications on small businesses available in your area, similar to, for example, *Small talk* which is the monthly publication of the Leeds Small Business Association. This is a newsletter publicizing meetings and courses, providing news and information on changes in the law and local administration affecting small businesses, and providing local company profiles.

The franchise magazine (q) published by Franchise Development Services Ltd concentrates, as the name suggests, on a particular type of business. It contains a mixture of general articles on business administration and legal organization, and more specific articles on the performance of named businesses. There are advertisements (mostly aimed at prospective franchisees) and calendars of events and exhibitions. It is useful supplementary reading for those contemplating joining a franchise operation. More general periodicals of use are *Business success* (incorporating *What finance*) (monthly, Parkway Publications) aimed at encouraging small businesses 'to make their enterprising ideas take off and succeed'; *Small business confidential* (Stonehart Publications); and *Your business* (fortnightly; Your Business Magazine Ltd). There are regular small business sections in the *Guardian* (Mondays), *The Times* (Fridays) and the *Financial Times* (Tuesdays).

Periodical publications

Commercial magazine publishers and specialized trade and professional associations produce periodicals in every subject field, of course: building, catering, hairdressing, office practice, software development and so on, and the small business owner is likely to subscribe to or regularly consult the relevant titles for news, developments and ideas within the subject itself. Significant periodicals in the catering trade, for example, are *Catering*, *Catering & Hotel Management*, *Catering Times* and *The Publican*. Similar works in other fields can most easily be traced using *Willing's Press Guide* (annual).

7

Automation and the small business

Mary Bosticco in her book *Instant business letters* (Gower, 2nd edn, 1985) points out the appropriateness of word processors in creating, storing and merging standard business letters, and certainly a dedicated word processor or the word-processing function of a personal computer can enhance basic document management. A good basic guide is *Word processing*, Vera Hughes (Hodder & Stoughton, 1985) in the Teach Yourself series. There are many other good inexpensive paperback guides specifically on word processing. To start with, a small computer rather than just a dedicated word processor offers much more potential for development of systems, but this can be an area of considerable anxiety, uncertainty and expense. Background information on finding the right system for the required tasks can be found in books, and one of the best introductions is Brenda Wroe's *Successful computing in a small business* (National Computing Centre, 1987). The author introduces the role and basic concepts of computers, then looks at applications in specific areas such as finance, management information and determining business requirements. There is a section on selecting and implementing systems, illustrated by case studies. *So you think your business needs a computer*, by Khalid Aziz (Kogan Page, 1986) is a brief introductory work that helps assess whether a computer will benefit a particular situation and what the cost will be. It covers the basic applications in accounts and filing. Many books along these lines

Automation and the small business

exist. Frank Blewett's *Beginner's guide to microcomputers* (Newnes Technical, 1985) is no longer right up to date, but the principles remain valid. It is aimed at the small business user and has a chapter on each application, for example, office work, stock control and accounts. The presentation is quite technical. *Introducing microcomputers in business*, B. Pannell (Hodder & Stoughton, rev. edn, 1985) in the Teach Yourself series, also examines the pros and cons of using a computer, asking why buy? how? and buy what? It is written for the novice and is sufficiently general not to date, although the chapter on suppliers and sources of advice may need updating. David Harvey examines a wider range of electronic services in *The electronic office in the smaller business* (Gower and Philips Business Systems, 1986). It is written in a largely non-technical style and covers the use of computers, word processors, electronic mail, online information services, viewdata and telex. There are case studies and lists of training organizations and consultants. Like the other books mentioned so far, it is not a buyer's trade guide, so shouldn't date too quickly. Other useful titles are *Small business computer systems*, Alan Clark (Hodder & Stoughton, 1987) and *How to choose microcomputers and software for your business*, Paul Beck (Telegraph Publications, rev. edn, 1988). The first looks at applications and methods through case studies and is very practical. It is written for BTEC students but will serve those in business. The aim of the second is to help the first-time buyer avoid the pitfalls. Anthony Meier's *Guide to microcomputer software for business* (Kogan Page, 1988) looks at the available software and its uses, including desk-top publishing and graphics.

8

The legal requirements

Small businesses are subject to a very large number of legal and financial constraints; it has been a feature of the encouragement of personal enterprise that 'red tape' should be minimized, and the atmosphere of encouragement has made it much more straightforward for a small business to be established; however, it still remains necessary to consider many regulations, and some essential legally-based decisions have to be taken at a planning stage. These can be summarized as:

1. the legal form the business is to take;
2. choice of premises;
3. trading and licensing regulations;
4. insurance of the business;
5. possible employment of staff;
6. health and safety requirements;
7. Inland Revenue taxation regulations;
8. VAT considerations;
9. patents, copyright, trade mark and design protection.

The most comprehensive overall guide is Patricia Clayton's *Law for the small business* (Kogan Page, 5th edn, 1987) in the *Daily Telegraph* Guide series: this contains a valuable preface and introductory chapter, pointing out what is at stake in setting up a business, what is required, and how to protect yourself and your business. Notes throughout the book refer to case law and give references to statutes. Towards the end of the volume, Chapter 13 explains the working of the legal machine (in England and Wales) which can clarify activities required and explain the motives for various actions. Appendices give addresses of organizations that could be of value, such as ACAS (the Advisory, Conciliation and Arbitration Service), the Registry of County Court Judgments, the Patent Office and Trade Mark Registry. A glossary of terms is provided, and several pages of draft pleadings – the style and form of presenting your case to an opponent or to a Court.

FORM OF THE BUSINESS

The decision on whether to begin as a sole trader or in partnership or within a cooperative or as a limited company is sometimes very clear (one person working alone would almost certainly start as a sole trader and might consider alternatives at a later date, depending on progress and future prospects); for others, partnerships or limited company status might seem equally feasible, and the legal background must be fully explored before a decision is taken.

Many of the basic guides tackle this question; Maurice Anslow's *Working for yourself* (Ward Lock, 1987) offers a concise and clear explanation, but information given is brief and not expanded, consequently much thought and calculation should be applied to the basics given. *Starting your own business* (Consumers' Association, rev. edn, 1987) (a Which? Book) also covers this adequately, and includes sound information on cooperatives (which are often treated very briefly or ignored), on franchising and on buying an existing business. For each form of business the data supplied is full and clear and includes notes of where further advice can be obtained.

Michel Syrett and Chris Dunn's *Starting a business on a shoestring* (Penguin Books, 1988) gives case studies in support of each form of business, with examples of typical trading activities, and offers lists of the advantages and disadvantages of each type in comparison with the others; this is a useful method of presentation, and each chapter concludes with a summary of the 'learning points' made. Colin Barrow's *Small business guide* (BBC

Publications, rev. edn, 1984) devotes several pages of Section 7 to the pros and cons of various business forms, and is competent in summarizing the situation.

Clive Woodcock's *Guardian guide to running a small business* (Kogan Page, 6th edn, 1987) has useful sections in chapters 2 and 4 on the formation and financing of cooperatives; John Pearce's *Running your own cooperative: a guide to the setting up of worker and community owned enterprises* (Kogan Page, 1984) in the Working for yourself series, covers this form of business in all its aspects, including the initial decisions needed and the legal structure that should be formed.

CHOICE OF PREMISES

Many small businesses will be started in domestic premises, and for some enterprises this will remain adequate. Extensions to houses can provide an economical means of obtaining space and avoid the burden of too great a capital debt. For many trades, high street or specialized premises are essential, and as businesses grow, houses may become increasingly unsuitable. Planning permission may be necessary for certain types of trade, and use of your home is probably unlikely to be approved if your trade is noisy, smelly or involves frequent deliveries and collections; local authority planning departments will give guidance. Clive Woodcock's *Guardian guide to running a small business* (Kogan Page, 6th edn, 1987) has a good section on business premises, and covers leasing and renting as alternatives to purchase. Patricia Clayton's *Law for the small business* (Kogan Page, 5th edn, 1987) has a comprehensive chapter on premises, citing relevant legislation, including health and safety requirements.

Peter Levene's *How to start and run your own shop* (Graham & Trotman, 2nd edn, 1988) offers very detailed and complete advice on retailing, covering choice of premises, planning consent required and other legal points. Howard Green's *How to choose business premises: a guide for the small firm* (Kogan Page, 1986) is a good introduction to the whole subject: regulations relating to premises are summarized; fire, safety and planning considerations outlined; leasing, renting and other bases of acquisition are discussed. Paul Chaplin's *Choosing and using professional advisers* (Kogan Page, rev. edn, 1986) covers premises in Chapter 6 ('other services available'), recommending use of specialist advice, but concisely summarizing the points to consider in choosing premises and the legal requirements that must be borne in mind.

TRADING AND LICENSING REGULATIONS

Many regulations apply to certain types of business, and the advice of a solicitor and the local authority planning department should be considered essential before any service is offered to the public. Retailing and the handling of food are particularly scrutinized. Health and safety are major considerations, and various laws apply to offices, shops and factories; food hygiene, public health and fire regulations apply to catering and hotel businesses; mobile shops, street traders and certain types of employment agencies require licences, as do scrap metal dealers, dairies, hairdressers and barbers, and manufacturers of some foodstuffs. Opening hours are regulated; dangerous toys are banned – there is no adequate published summary of all regulations relating to all business activity, and it must be seen as essential to contact the local authority Chief Trading Standards Officer, the Environmental Health Department or the local police if there is any possible doubt as to what is required; using a solicitor would be a worthwhile expense. Patricia Clayton's *Law for the small business* (Kogan Page, 5th edn, 1987) offers a summary of some of the regulations likely to be encountered, and most of the general guides make some mention of them, but care should be taken. *Starting your own business* (Consumers' Association, rev. edn, 1987) gives good coverage of retailing law.

INSURANCE

A small business set up from home must be covered by insurance, as normal domestic policies exclude damage or loss caused by business activity. Insurance companies will generally extend policies to cover 'safe' trades, but some types of trade may need special cover for fire, burglary and public liability, and it may also be necessary to adjust motor policies if a car is also to be used for business purposes. Chapter 7 of Patricia Clayton's book can be recommended as a full, general guide; Maurice Anslow's *Working for yourself* (Ward Lock, 1987) deals briefly but adequately with the topic (Chapter 14), and Paul Chaplin's *Choosing and using professional advisers* (Kogan Page, rev. edn, 1986) offers advice on how to use insurance brokers and companies to your best advantage. Most of the other general guides we have mentioned offer basic advice on what is strictly necessary and what should be seen as desirable minimum cover.

EMPLOYMENT OF STAFF

Small businesses usually begin as one-person, or one-person and spouse, enterprises. In partnerships and cooperatives all participants are of equal status, but sooner or later in most small businesses the question of employing staff is raised. The legal background to this topic is formidable and needs to be handled with great care to avoid friction, bad feeling or time-consuming and expensive redress.

An ideal initial guide is *Employing people: the ACAS handbook for small firms* (Advisory, Conciliation and Arbitration Service, 1987); amongst the sections of this booklet, which is clearly and simply written, are several relating to the legal aspects of employing staff. Section 3 deals with the employment contract, Section 6 with rules and procedures, Section 7 with unfair dismissal, and Section 10 with employee representation. Each section begins with a series of key questions; for example, Section 3 highlights: what is an employment contract?; does an employment contract have to be in writing?; what are express and implied terms?; what are employees' statutory rights?; how can a contract be altered?; how can a contract be ended? Each of the questions is answered in the section, with examples of forms of words, reference to official publications, leaflets from government departments, publications of the Equal Opportunities Commission, the Commission for Racial Equality and other ACAS publications and Code of Practice leaflets. The booklet concludes with contact addresses for ACAS, lists of publications and addresses of other relevant organizations.

Other government assistance is issued by the Department of Employment in the Employment Legislation series, a set of

The legal requirements

booklets outlining the legal requirements on employers and the rights of employees. Each title is regularly revised and at present comprises 16 booklets:

1. Written statement of main terms and conditions of employment.
2. Procedure for handling redundancies.
3. Employee's rights on insolvency of employer.
4. Employment rights for the expectant mother.
5. Suspension on medical grounds under health and safety regulations.
6. Facing redundancy? – time off for job hunting or to arrange training.
7. Union membership rights and the closed shop including the union-labour-only provisions of the Employment Act 1982.
8. Itemized pay statements.
9. Guarantee payments.
10. Employment rights on the transfer of an undertaking.
11. Rules governing continuous employment and a week's pay.
12. Time off for public duties.
13. Unfairly dismissed?
14. Rights to notice and reasons for dismissal.
15. Union secret ballots.
16. Redundancy payments.

The Inland Revenue issues guidance leaflets to employers relating to the taxation of employees; leaflet IR53, for instance, is entitled *Thinking of taking someone on?* (Inland Revenue, 1988) and explains the Pay-As-You-Earn (PAYE) system. Such publications can be obtained from the Small Firms Service, from Jobcentres or Tax Offices. National Insurance leaflets can be obtained from main post offices and local Social Security (DHSS) offices.

Published guides to small business operation usually cover the basics of employment legislation; *Starting your own business* (Consumers' Association, rev. edn, 1987) devotes a chapter to 'How to be an employer' and explains employee rights at length. Michel Syrett and Chris Dunn's *Starting a business on a shoestring* (Penguin Books, 1988) offers a clear and concise summary of statutory legal obligations, and recommends contact with your legal adviser before taking on any member of staff. Patricia

Clayton (*Law for the small business*) covers employment law in her Chapter 8, and this can be recommended as a good outline. The chapter 'Employing people' by Shelagh Sweeney in Clive Woodcock's *Guardian guide to running a small business* devotes most of its contents to questions of dismissal and lay-off.

Fuller summaries of employment law are available in abbreviated legal textbooks; Colin Thomas's *Employment law* (Hodder & Stoughton, 1984) in the Teach Yourself series deals with contracts, employers' duties, safety, wages and dismissal; Greville Janner's *Practical guide to the Employment Act 1980 – industrial relations and employment law* (Business Books, 1980) is very comprehensive and gives over 150 pages of appendices, being extracts of laws, codes of practice and statutory regulations.

Len Collinson and Christopher Hodkinson's *Employment law keynotes* (Colgran Publications, 1985) also provides a sound survey and features useful appendices of specimen forms and codes of practice. Croner's *Reference book for employers* (Croner Publications; loose leaf, monthly updates) offers a reliable and extensive synopsis of current legislation covering all aspects of employment law and practice. A useful section relates to EEC requirements.

HEALTH AND SAFETY

All people at work have a duty to be concerned about health and safety; this applies equally to employers, employees and the self-employed. The basic law is the Health and Safety at Work Act 1974, with certain types of premises also covered by the Offices, Shops and Railway Premises Act 1963 and the Factories Act 1961. The co-ordinating body for regulations is the Health and Safety Executive (HSE), and local authorities have an enforcement role. HSE publishes booklets outlining its activities, the regulations to be observed and pads of forms for notifying accidents, etc. The Reporting of Injuries, Diseases and Dangerous Occurrences Regulations 1985 (RIDDOR) took effect in 1986 and cover employers' duties to report all such incidents. HSE information is also available via an online service – HSELINE – and on a CD-ROM format.

HSE has 21 area offices throughout the United Kingdom and three designated public enquiry points:

St Hugh's House, Stanley Precinct,
Trinity Road,
Bootle, Merseyside L20 3QY.
Telephone: 051–951 4381

Broad Lane, Sheffield S3 7HQ.
Telephone: 0742 752539

Baynards House, 1 Chepstow Place,
Westbourne Grove, London W2 4TF.
Telephone 01–221–0870

Most aspects of HSE requirements are explained in their *Essentials of health and safety at work* (HMSO, 1988) which is excellently presented, with numerous checklists, diagrams and case studies. This inexpensive publication should be an essential purchase for any small business. A good discussion of this aspect is given in Humphrey Norvill's chapter 'Health and safety' in Clive Woodcock's *Guardian guide to running a small business* (Kogan Page, 6th edn, 1987).

INLAND REVENUE AND NATIONAL INSURANCE REQUIREMENTS

All businesses are obliged to make tax returns, and the individual liabilities of employers, employees, partners or cooperative members are discussed more fully in Chapters 3 and 4 where self-help guides are analysed. Although guides tend to concentrate on means by which advantages can be maximized, there is obviously a legal requirement to organize personal and business tax affairs in an efficient manner, to provide accurate and timely returns; hence the inclusion of the topic here.

In addition to the self-help guides, most popular books on tax planning offer basic advice on what is needed from a business. W. J. Sinclair's *Allied Dunbar tax guide 1987–88* (Longman, 1987) devotes four chapters to this; Chapter 9 discusses employment income and PAYE, with details of fringe benefits, allowances, cars, assets and directors' fees; a further chapter looks at business and professional income, including profits and losses, expenses and stock valuation, and is illustrated with clear tables, examples and

Setting up in Business

references to relevant legislation; Chapter 11 refers to partnerships and the following chapter to the taxation position of companies.

The *Which? book of tax* (Hodder & Stoughton, 2nd edn, 1987) also provides comprehensive details, illustrated with numerous examples and tables; for those starting in a very small way, this book offers good advice on spare-time income and employment of family members in part-time capacities, although coverage of the whole range of business requirements is included. Mavis Seymour and Stephen Say's *Stoy Hayward business tax guide* (Kogan Page, 1988) can also be commended for its clear division of tax matters into 27 well laid-out, concise chapters, with appendices showing specimen Inland Revenue forms. Cooper and Lybrand's *Tax saving for your business* (Kogan Page, 7th edn, 1987) offers a question-and-answer format, easy to follow and comprehensive in coverage.

Tax guides that concentrate on self-employed people include Bill Packer and Colin Sandy's *Touche Ross tax guide for the self-employed* (Papermac, 3rd edn, 1987), effectively and clearly written, and Ian Hill's *Tax and the self-employed* (Daily Telegraph, 1988). All these guides offer advice on how to operate PAYE and National Insurance tables for employees, and this is the special area covered in Carol Anderson's *PAYE: a working guide for the small business* (Daily Telegraph, 1988). *Earning money at home* (Hodder & Stoughton and the Consumers' Association, 1986) gives information on the tax situation as it applies to home-based people. *Tax saving for your business 1988/89* (Kogan Page, 1988) and the *Allied Dunbar business tax and law guide* (Longman, 1988) are also valuable sources.

VAT

Value Added Tax is a favourite topic for complaint amongst small businesses; the tax guides already cited in this chapter cover the VAT requirements to a greater or lesser extent, and of course, local VAT offices can provide leaflets outlining obligations; the *Touche Ross tax guide for the self-employed* and the *Allied Dunbar tax guide* both offer full information on VAT and the latter illustrates this material with many examples.

A specialized source is Ian Hill's *VAT: a working guide for the small business* (Daily Telegraph/William Curtis, 1987) which gives a good introduction then deals in detail with the scheme, and quotes examples, specimen forms, trade classifications, etc. Croner's *Reference book for VAT* (Croner Publications, monthly updated loose-leaf format) is a substantial guide, providing up-to-date information on the whole area, quoting the VAT Act in full, giving many tables and lists, relevant additional finance Acts, Statutory Instruments and a good index to make the data accessible. *Value-added tax: a practical guide for your business* (Kogan Page, 1988) can also be commended.

PATENTS, COPYRIGHT, TRADE MARKS AND REGISTERED DESIGNS

Businesses which are based on an original idea or invention, whether in manufacture, production or marketing, can be protected against competitors taking over the idea, 'passing off' their products or services as yours in a manner to mislead customers, or using your designs or product names without permission. Artistic, literary or musical creations can also be protected, as can trade marks. A problem arises because different countries have different rules; pursuing a claim anywhere can be expensive, and chances of success abroad are low and costs high – beyond the range of small businesses. The services of specialized advisers are recommended in instances where the unique idea is quite essential to the business and any infringement would be calamitous.

Some of the self-help guides cover these points, but many ignore them or offer only scant information. Paul Chaplin's *Choosing and using professional advisers* (Kogan Page, rev. edn, 1986) discusses the services of patent and trade mark agents, but does not include other such services. *Starting your own business* (Consumers' Association, rev. edn, 1987) contains a chapter on 'protecting your business idea', which covers patents, trade marks, service marks, registered designs and copyright; information is brief and concise. Colin Barrow's *Small business guide* (BBC Publications, rev. edn, 1984) also provides brief coverage and adds a list of appropriate organizations (pp. 269–74) for further information.

Patricia Clayton's *Law for the small business* (Kogan Page, 5th edn, 1987) contains in Chapter 11 a synopsis of 'intellectual property' – patents, copyrights and trade marks – which outlines

49

the EEC situation, patent protection, licensing patents, copyright, registered designs, trade marks and service marks. Computer programs are specifically mentioned, and the chapter also draws attention to the Data Protection Act 1984. There is also a discussion of typical problems and possible legal remedies. (New copyright legislation is currently being enacted in the UK; care should be taken to avoid depending on information relating to earlier legislation.) Legal textbooks cover this field, but at a level probably inappropriate for small businesses; however, two important titles are George Myrant's *Protection of industrial designs* (McGraw Hill, 1977), and Diana Guy and Guy Leigh's *The EEC and intellectual property* (Sweet and Maxwell, 1988).

IN CONCLUSION

There are several advanced legal textbooks covering each of the areas mentioned in this chapter; generally these are intended for the legal profession rather than the lay-person, and they are deliberately not included here. The commercial departments of local public libraries will have copies of most major titles, and these could be consulted for preliminary data on certain problems; consultation with specialist advisers may be seen as an awkward expense, but in a complex area it could make the difference between clear progress and a time-consuming, expensive muddle.

A number of titles are available written in a style that the business person can readily understand; Colin Thomas's *Company law* (Hodder & Stoughton, 2nd edn, 1985) in the 'Teach Yourself' series, provides material on the formation of a company, the duties of directors and handling of accounts. J. R. Lewis's *Law for the retailer and distributor* (Jordans, 3rd edn, 1979) discusses the law of contract, sale of goods, consumer credit, consumer protection and employment law. *Handbook of consumer law* (Consumers' Association, 2nd edn, 1986) Which? Books series, examines topics such as fair trading, defective goods, defective services, trade descriptions, pricing policy, consumer safety and food hygiene.

An essential, comprehensive source is Croner's *Reference book for the self-employed and smaller business* (Croner Publications, updated monthly in a loose-leaf binder); a substantial guide of over 600 pages, constantly up to date with each page clearly showing its

The legal requirements

issue date, and concluding with a 50-page index, this source provides detailed information on taxation, VAT, National Insurance, employment law, health and safety, consumer law and company law. This publication needs to be used with care to ensure that the updates have been correctly inserted and old material removed. Its comprehensiveness and currency make it the ideal final source for checking regulations.

9

Further sources of advice and support

Throughout this book we have mentioned self-help guides to setting up in business and discussed many sources which offer information and help. It is apparent that although there is substantial support available, advisory and financial, the sources are numerous, the purposes various and there is an inevitable feeling that money is being thrown at a problem without clear guidelines and criteria. The problem is one of many sources of help, governmental, local governmental, charitable, commercial, self-help and so on, offering various means of support and targeting piecemeal businesses and potential businesses of all sorts of sizes and types. The result is that although considerable support is available, the framework for discovering what support, for what purpose, for what size, in which areas, is simply not adequate. The business consultants Segal Quince Wicksteed sponsored by the Department of Employment, Barclays Bank and English Estates, highlight the confusion, duplication and possible waste of the present system in their study *Encouraging small business start-up and growth: creating a supportive local environment* (HMSO, 1988). The report also questions the value of some of the help offered and suggests that if too much free advice is available, businesses will be unwilling to use specialist services when necessary.

Further sources of advice and support

GOVERNMENT SERVICES

The Department of Employment is keenly promoting the services of its key agency in this field, the Small Firms Service (SFS); SFS operates from a number of centres throughout Great Britain (Figure 9.1) and can be contacted by dialling 100 and asking for Freefone Enterprise. The SFS issues a large number of booklets, free of charge, which outline the opportunities, problems and strategies appropriate to small business; an introductory booklet *Starting your own business – the practical steps* provides basic advice on all aspects, and the SFS offers several similar brief introductions to marketing, accounting, franchising and similar topics.

A recent innovation from SFS is the *National reference book* (1988), a database of small business information aimed at advisory bodies, arranged into over 100 subject fields and intended to co-ordinate and update the whole advisory scene. The headquarters of the SFS (Steel House, Tothill St, London SW1H 9NF) carries full details of all publications, as do the regional centres.

Advisory consultations are also offered by the SFS for those with plans who need advice in confidence, and for those with problems who need support and help. The initial meetings are available free and further sessions are offered for a modest fee. The SFS Business Development Service provides facts on local or national markets, industry structure, distribution, supply, exporting, market research and numerous other related topics; this service aims to help newly established firms to grow, and the advice is completely impartial, confidential and non-interfering.

The Department of Trade and Industry (DTI) represents the other major government initiative on small businesses; the 'department for Enterprise' is offering advice and support to further good business practice with a view to successful competition in the 1992 European single market. The Enterprise Initiative consists of several programmes – free business reviews by experienced counsellors; specialized consultancy at assisted cost into marketing, quality, design, planning, finance and information systems; enterprise grants in development areas; research and technology initiatives; the Small Firms Merit Award for Research and Technology (SMART); a business and education initiative based on a network of Regional Technology Centres; an export initiative; and inner-city initiatives. The DTI schemes are co-

Birmingham: Small Firms Centre, 9th Floor, Alpha Tower, Suffolk Street, Queensway, Birmingham B1 1TT, tel. 021-643 33344.

Bristol: Small Firms Centre, 6th Floor, The Pithay, Bristol BS1 2NB, tel 0272 294546.

Cambridge: Small Firms Centre, Carlyle House, Carlyle Road, Cambridge CB4 3DN, tel 0223-63312.

Cardiff: Small Firms Centre, 16 St David's House, Wood Street, Cardiff CF1 1ER, tel 0222-396116.

Edinburgh: Small Firms Centre, Rosebery House, Haymarket Terrace, Edinburgh EH12 5EZ, tel 031-337 9229.

Glasgow: Small Firms Centre, 21 Bothwell Street, Glasgow G2 6NR, tel 041-248 6014.

Leeds: Small Firms Centre, 1 Park Row, City Square, Leeds LS1 5NR, tel 0532-445151.

Liverpool: Small Firms Centre, Graeme House, Derby Square, Liverpool L2 7UJ, tel 051-236 5756.

London: Small Firms Centre, Ebury Bridge House, 2-18 Ebury Bridge Road, London SW1W 8QD, tel 01-730 8451.

Manchester: Small Firms Centre, 26-28 Deansgate, Manchester M3 1RH, tel 061-832 5282.

Newcastle: Small Firms Centre, Centro House, 3 Cloth Market, Newcastle upon Tyne, NE1 6PZ, tel 091-232 5353.

Nottingham: Small Firms Centre, Severns House, 20 Middle Pavement, Nottingham NG1 7DW, tel. 0602-581205.

Reading: Small Firms Centre, Abbey Hall, Abbey Square, Reading RG1 3BE, tel. 0734-591733.

Stevenage: Small Firms Centre, Business and Technology Centre, Bessemer Drive, Stevenage, Herts 8G1 2DX.

Figure 9.1 Small firms centres operated through the Department of Employment

ordinated from regional offices (Figure 9.2) and up-to-date information on activities is available in its bi-monthly newspaper *In business now*.

NATIONAL AGENCIES

Many support services are available nationally, and details apply in various ways in different areas. A major programme of industrial regeneration is operated by some national undertakings that have contracted, leaving vacant sites, skilled workforces and high unemployment; the principal examples of these schemes are those run by British Coal and British Steel. Details are available either from the bodies themselves or from local advice centres in the areas to which they apply. The support offered will usually be a package of premises, advice, financial assistance, retraining and liaison with local services.

English Estates was originally a government-funded agency set up to renovate services in areas of industrial dereliction, offering advice and support as well as premises and sites. Business support services are usually confined to directing clients to local agencies in the areas, not seeking to duplicate existing successful arrangements.

Action Resource Centres are a regional network of offices which bring together concerned and experienced individuals from the business world and make their expertise available to those in the community who need advice and support to set up in self-employment or to start up small firms. ARC's central office will provide details of their facilities (Henrietta House, 9 Henrietta Place, London W1M 9AG Tel: 01-629-3826).

In rural areas the Rural Development Commission, widely known by its earlier name CoSIRA (Council for Small Industries in Rural Areas) offers an excellent, proven service; courses and training are available, together with management advice, financial advice in cooperation with other organizations, free initial consultations or site surveys, and some loan assistance. RDC services are available in country areas and in towns with a population below 10,000. The central office is at 141 Castle St, Salisbury, Wilts SP1 3TP Tel: 0722 336255.

The National Federation of Self-Employed and Small Businesses

North east
Stanegate House, 2 Groat Market, Newcastle-upon-Tyne
NE1 1YN, tel 091-232 4722, telex 53178

North west
Sunley Tower, Piccadilly Plaza, Manchester M1 4BA
tel 061-236 2171, telex 667104

Yorkshire and Humberside
Priestley House, Park Row, Leeds LS1 5LF, tel 0532 443171, telex 557925

East midlands
Severns House, 20 Middle Pavement, Nottingham NG1 7PW, tel 0602 506181, telex 37143

West midlands
Ladywood House, Stephenson Street, Birmingham B2 4DT, tel 021-632 4111, telex 337919

South east
Ebury Bridge House, Ebury Bridge Road, London SW1W 8QD, tel 01-730 9678, telex 297124

South west
The Pithay, Bristol BS1 2PB, tel 0272 272666, telex 44214

Scotland
Scottish Office
Industry Department for Scotland, Alhambra House, 45 Waterloo Street, Glasgow G2 6AT, tel 41-248 2855, telex 777883

Wales
Welsh Office
Industry Department, New Crown Building, Cathays Park, Cardiff CF1 3NQ, tel 0222 825396, telex 498228

Northern Ireland
Industrial Development Board for Northern Ireland
IDB House, 64 Chichester Street, Belfast BT1 4JX, tel 0232 233233, telex 747025

Figure 9.2 Department of Trade and Industry Offices offering information on DTI services for small firms

is an organization set up to offer advice to its members and to lobby local and national government for greater efficiency in handling the needs of small businesses. Details of membership and the services available are obtainable from the NFSE central office, 140 Lower Marsh, London SE1 7AE Tel: 01-928-9272. Other business associations which may offer specialist support can be found listed by Colin Barrow in *The small business guide* (BBC Publications, rev. edn, 1984, pp. 76–82).

COMMERCIAL ASSISTANCE

Provision of capital to small businesses is a flourishing part of the operations of most banks; the advice of bank managers and other specialist bank staff has long been highly regarded, and competition between organizations to provide funds has led banks to offer an excellent back-up service of advice and helpful background publications. Most banks issue regular digests or magazines publicizing their small-business services and giving case-histories of successful ventures. Cooperation between the self-employed or small business and their bank is an essential component of a good business future; the bank will provide support and advice whilst a business plan is prepared to their satisfaction, and will then advise and monitor progress.

Development capital groups, venture capital providers and financial trusts will offer similar packages of cash and advice. Details of which organizations are active, and what they offer, are publicized regularly in business periodicals or financial journals such as *Investors' Chronicle*.

ENTERPRISE AGENCIES AND SCIENCE PARKS

Over the last decade, the number of enterprise agencies in the UK has grown from a handful to over 160; the agencies are non-profit-making companies coordinating local and national organizations that offer support and sponsorship. Services may include business clubs, training activities, courses, advisory workshops and a network of linked services from local authorities, chambers of commerce, colleges, commercial firms and other advisory bodies.

Setting up in Business

Local offices of the Small Firms Service, local authority enterprise offices and other advice agencies will give details of the local enterprise agencies. Michel Syrett and Chris Dunn list the agencies on a regional basis in *Starting a business on a shoestring* (Penguin, 1988, pages 236–49), and a directory is issued by Business in the Community (227A City Road, London EC1V 1JU Tel: 01-253-3716). The agencies usually have an educational or training role and may also be encountered in following up courses mentioned in Chapter 2.

Premises for small businesses are readily available in certain parts of the country, enterprise zones or areas where industrial decline makes it desirable to attract new firms. Local services already mentioned will provide details of packages available and the financial inducements offered. For high-technology firms, locations in science parks can offer the advantages of scientific support; members of the UK Science Park Association are listed by Syrett and Dunn, pp. 256–8. Commonsense, useful advice for those considering business tenancies is offered in Michael Malone's *Practical guide for business tenants* (Ross Anderson, 1986); for retail premises, sound help is given in A. St J. Price's *Buying a Shop* (Kogan Page, 3rd edn, 1986), a *Daily Telegraph* guide.

LOCAL AUTHORITY SERVICES

Local authority small business initiatives are many and various; in the great majority of cases, help is channelled through the relevant local enterprise agency, but many authorities offer small-scale support, advice and assistance, grants or interest relief for firms which can offer potential employment. This can benefit very small companies or the sole trader who needs some help but does not wish to undertake a large expansion plan.

OTHER LOCAL SUPPORT

Local business ventures and enterprise agencies issue leaflets and publications which will draw attention to other local facilities that can benefit small businesses. These may be training providers, business services, local colleges or local small-business associations;

such organizations are a valuable means of discovering further support, sharing problems and experience and keeping in touch with local developments.

FACTS AND FIGURES

The essential reference sources have been discussed in Chapter 5, and the purpose of this section is to mention some advisory volumes that may help in the day-to-day running of a small enterprise. Necessary basic background details on all aspects of small firm management, training, office services, purchase and supply, distribution, expansion, etc. form a part of the *Business fact finder* (Kogan Page, 1987) which is over 540 pages in length, well indexed, and gives summaries, tables and checklists.

Duties of company directors are outlined in *Being a director: a guide to the responsibilities and opportunities* (Kogan Page, 1988), while the company secretary's role is explained in A. J. Scrine's *Be your own company secretary* (Kogan Page and Institute of Chartered Accountants, 1987). Financial control of the enterprise can be improved by the use of guide books such as *Harrap's dictionary of business and finance* (Harrap, 1988), Colin Barrow's *Financial management for the small business* (Kogan Page, 2nd edn, 1988), or at the simplest level by using practical book-keeping texts, for example, Paul Ordidge's *Simple cash books for small businesses* (Kogan Page, 1986), J. R. Stott's *Basic accounting* (Hodder & Stoughton, 1985) a Teach Yourself book, or Max Pullen's *Do your own book-keeping* (Kogan Page, 1988). Section 5 'Financial preparation and control' in the *Lloyds Bank small business guide* (Penguin Books, 1987) contains some excellent material on balance sheet forecasts, monitoring financial performances and keeping adequate records of everything that you will need to recall to plot financial progress.

Office routines, telephone costs, letter writing and other administrative activities that will multiply as a small firm begins to expand can be controlled and improved with handbooks such as Penny Hackett's *Success in office practice* (J. Murray, 1984) which includes basic ideas on filing, stationery, communication and the prospect of the 'paperless office', or Peter Brunt's *How to cut your business costs* (Kogan Page, 1988) which examines backroom economies. Correspondence can be operated speedily with Mary Bosticco's *Instant business letters* (Gower, 2nd edn, 1985) discussed in Chapter 3.

PENSIONS FOR THE SELF-EMPLOYED

The self-employed have had a wide range of choice over personal pension schemes for several years; changes in 1988 have affected pension arrangements for all categories of employed people, and it is very important to consult only recent guides to find absolutely up-to-date information. There is no shortage of pension guides and many life insurance handbooks also include advice on pensions; many such titles are updated regularly and so the recent changes will be incorporated in them fairly rapidly. John Wilson and Bryn Davies's *Your new pensions choice* (Tolley, 3rd edn, 1988), or John and Carmel Wilson's *Guide to pensions and life assurance* (Kogan Page, 1988) would be good introductions, but similar titles abound.

SUPPORT FOR YOUNG PEOPLE

Although most of the schemes to encourage enterprise are applicable to people of any age, some specialized schemes have appeared which are targeted at young people, generally below the age of 25. The Youth Enterprise Scheme and the Youth Business Initiative were established programmes that have now merged to form the Prince's Youth Business Trust (PYBT); the Trust awards bursaries (not loans) of up to £1000 that can be spent on training, tools, equipment, insurance or transport, but not for capital expenditure or rent of premises. A sound business plan must be prepared, and the advice of local Trust nominees has to be accepted. Loans of up to £5000 are available to applicants referred from enterprise agencies or another advisory organization.

Many small-scale local authority schemes are aimed principally at the young unemployed or newly self-employed, and local enterprise agencies will provide details of what is available in your area. National schemes are also operated by banks, finance houses and large companies; programmes such as Livewire and Head Start

Further sources of advice and support

are sponsored by industry but operate through their own administrations. Clive Woodcock's *Guardian guide to running a small business* (Kogan Page, 6th edn, 1987) and Appendix 5 of Michel Syrett and Chris Dunn's *Starting a business on a shoestring* (Penguin Books, 1988) carry details of the major schemes; Colin Barrow's *Small business guide* (BBC Publications, rev. edn, 1984) also describes various organizations in Section 9, but some of this information is now out of date.

SELF-EMPLOYED DISABLED PEOPLE

Mary Thompson's *Employment for disabled people* (Kogan Page, 1986) is an excellent summary of all aspects of the work prospects of the disabled. Chapter 8 is entitled 'Running your own business' and discusses the suitability of various types of work, the help that is available and the other considerations that must be met. Some ideas of the type of work that could be undertaken are given; the general self-help guides give little specific information on the special help that the disabled can expect.

SUPPORT FOR COOPERATIVES

The Careers and Occupational Information Centre (COIC) issue a Job Outline (no. 61) *Worker cooperatives* which gives basic information on the support available and the addresses of relevant organizations. A good all-round guide, although now rather out of date, is John Pearce's *Running your own cooperative: a guide to the setting up of worker and community owned enterprises* (Kogan Page, 1984); this covers the whole field, but includes sections on sources of advice and on information sources, listing nearly 30 titles.

PROFESSIONAL ADVISERS

The self-employed and small firms are often reluctant to use specialist advice because of the likely cost; it must be doubted whether this is a good policy: professional advisers will give ideas and opinions on the operation of a business from their experience that may avoid or prevent problems and expenses as the business grows. Administration is time-consuming, and as a business expands and develops its proprietor or director will find little opportunity to spend hours on this, rather than on improvement of the product, service or marketing activities.

Most of the self-help guides have something to say about using an accountant or solicitor; the fullest general synopsis is Paul Chaplin's *Choosing and using professional advisers* (Kogan Page, rev. edn, 1986). The introduction explains why the use of a specialist adviser can be a good investment and discusses the range of support available. Various chapters examine the services of accountants, bank managers, other financial services such as credit arrangements, leasing and factoring, the role of solicitors and specialist advisers in the areas of property, insurance, marketing, exporting, management, staffing, patents and office automation.

Each chapter describes what the specialist does, how to choose an appropriate person, what the charges are, and how to use the specialist to greatest effect at lowest cost. Summaries of 'dos and don'ts' are given at the end of each chapter, and the final chapter and appendices give ideas for further advice from organizations and specialized publications.

Index

Accounts 25–6
Action Resource Centres 55
Advertising 23–4
Automation 38–9

Book-keeping 25–6, 59
Business Enterprise Programme (BEP) 9–10
Business plans 20–21

Careers and Occupational Information Centre (COIC) publications 11, 13, 61
Case studies 17
Chambers of Commerce 36
Computers 38–9
Cooperatives 17, 18–19, 41, 61
Copyright 49–50
CoSIRA 11, 55
Courses, educational and training 7–13

Debt collection 26

Department of Employment
 Publications 6, 9, 26, 34–5, 44–5
 Training initiatives 6
 Small Firms Services 9, 34–5, 53, 58
Department of Trade and Industry 53–4, 56
 Publications 34
Dictionaries 30–31
Directories 31–3
Disabled persons, employment 61

Employment law 44–6
Encyclopaedias 30–31
English Estates 55
Enterprise Allowance Scheme (EAS) 9
Enterprise in Higher Education (EHE) 5–6
Enterprise Initiative 53

Financial administration 25–6, 38–9, 59–60

Financial support 9, 21, 57
Firmstart 10
Franchises 17, 18–19, 36, 41
Freelance opportunities 15, 16

Graduate Enterprise
  Programme (GEP) 6, 10
Graduate Gateway Programme
  (GGP) 6, 10

Handbooks 32–3
Head Start 60–61
Health and safety at work 22–3, 43, 46–7
Home-based opportunities 17–18, 27–8

Insurance 43–4

Law *see* Legal requirements
Legal requirements 22–3, 40–51
Licensing regulations 43
Livewire 60–61
Loan Guarantee Scheme 9
Local authorities 32, 58, 60

Management 24–6, 38–9, 59–60
Management Extension
  Programme 10
Manpower Services
  Commission *see* Training
  Agency
Manufacturing 23
Market research 21–2
Marketing 22

National Federation of Self-
  Employed and Small
  Businesses 35, 55–7
National Insurance 45, 47–8

New Enterprise Programme
  (NEP) 10

Office administration 24–6, 38–9

Part-time opportunities 15, 17–18
Patents 49–50
Pay-As-You-Earn (PAYE) 45, 47–8
Pensions 60
Periodicals 34–7, 57
PICKUP 7–8
Premises 22–3, 42–3, 58
Prince's Youth Business Trust
  (PYBT) 60
Private Enterprise Programme
  (PEP) 10
Professional advisers 61–2
Project Fullemploy 13
Publicity 23–4
Purchase and supply 23, 59

Registered designs 49–50
Rural Development
  Commission 11, 55

Science parks 58
Self-employment opportunities 27–9
Small business clubs and
  associations 35–6, 58
Small Firms Service 9, 34–5, 53, 58
SMART 53
Staff employment 44–6

Taxation 45, 47–9
Trade marks 49–50

Index

Trading regulations 43
Training Access Points (TAPs) 8
Training Agency 5–6, 9–11
Training Commission *see* Training Agency
'Training for Enterprise' programme 9

Value added tax (VAT) 48–9

Vocational Education and Training Group (VET) 10–11, 12

Women and self-employment 16

Youth Business Initiative 60
Youth Enterprise Scheme 60
Youth schemes 16, 60–61